DAN CASEY + GRIFFIN BRAND

BRING YOUR OWN PENCIL

BILL WALSH'S PLAYBOOK
FOR *WINNING* AT *ANYTHING*

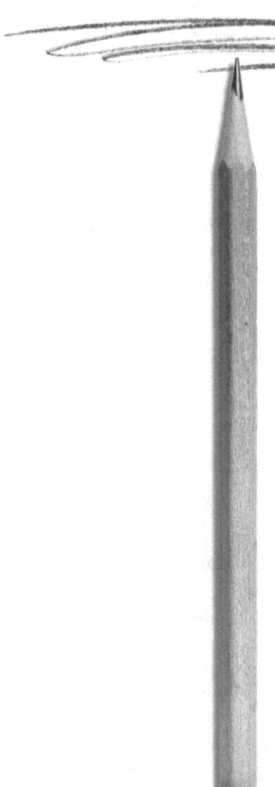

GRIDIRON PRESS

How this Book was Built

SECTION TWO: THE PROCESS

SECTION THREE: THE PEOPLE

POST GAME

Bring Your Own Pencil

"Character is contagious."

- **BILL WALSH**

"The fight is won or lost far away from the witnesses, behind the lines, in the gym, and out there on the road; long before I dance under those lights."

- **MUHAMMAD ALI**

"It's not the will to win that matters — everyone has that. It's the will to prepare to win that matters."

- **PAUL "BEAR" BRYANT**

Bill Walsh was 47 years old when he finally earned his first NFL head coaching job. It had been a long, frustrating climb to get there. He had been overlooked by key decision-makers and passed over by mentors. But in 1979, with 25 years of coaching experience behind him and a wise-looking crop of white hair atop his head, Bill was named head coach of the San Francisco 49ers. He finally made it, and the game of football would never be the same.

By the time he arrived in San Francisco, Bill had accumulated decades of hard-won lessons and expertise. He came with a plan – a detailed, demanding process to rewrite the fortunes of a long-dormant franchise. At the center of that plan was what Bill called his "Standard of Performance," a clear expectation for how every person in the organization would think, prepare, and behave. Bill didn't just preach the standard, he lived it. His competitiveness and relentless attention to detail set the tone.

Bill quickly learned that he could not maintain the standard on his own. He needed to find like-minded individuals who shared his maniacal drive and commitment to preparation. If the 49ers were going to be great, the culture had to live beyond him.

> *"Running a football franchise is not unlike running any other business: You start first with a structural format and basic philosophy and then find the people who can implement it."*
>
> **- BILL WALSH**

Before the 1981 season, Bill became enamored with a free-agent, 11-year veteran linebacker named Jack "Hacksaw" Reynolds. Hacksaw earned his nickname years earlier at the University of Tennessee after being so upset following a loss that "he went to K-Mart and bought a hacksaw and twenty blades. He then proceeded to saw his '53 Chevy completely in half."

He was intense, volatile, and by NFL standards, past his prime. His previous team, the Los Angeles Rams, believed he was over the hill, despite the fact that he had just led the team in tackles. With his best years seemingly behind him, the Rams cut him loose. After a decade of plugging holes in the middle of the defense, his body was banged up, but his mind was sharp. And Bill decided he was just what the 49ers needed.

Bill wanted the "right kind of crazy" on his football team. Hacksaw was certainly a character, but beneath his brooding intensity was a maniacal commitment to film study and preparation. He famously brought his own projector to training camp so he could grind through tape long after coaches had gone home. Defensive coach George Seifert recalled, "At meetings, he'd sit down at a desk, and he had this big old box crammed full of his pencils and pencil sharpener, and he'd just go through them. He would sit there and write down everything." His study habits were on full display. No stone would be left unturned in his preparation. Bill knew his presence would set the standard for the young players on the 49ers' defense.

Hacksaw's lessons started immediately. Early in training camp, the highly touted draft pick, Ronnie Lott, leaned over during a meeting and asked Hacksaw if he could borrow a pencil. Hacksaw refused, telling the rookie that he wouldn't be a success in the league until he brought his own pencil to every meeting, so he'd better start now.

"Bring your own pencil" was a simple standard with far-reaching implications. Championship teams aren't built on talent alone. They're built on ownership. On personal responsibility for preparation and the understanding that every detail matters. Hacksaw's mentality permeated the young players, the veterans, and even the coaching staff. Lott was quickly transformed from a naive rookie to an integral contributor. Throughout his Hall of Fame career, Lott's preparation and relentless style of play helped lead the 49ers to four Super Bowl victories. In the grand scheme of his career, a pencil is barely a footnote, but the lesson had a profound impact.

"Hacksaw did a lot for this team," Lott remembered. "He created a lot of good habits for this organization. He taught a lot of people how to win."

Bring Your Own Pencil is about learning how to win.

It means taking responsibility for your own preparation. It means approaching your craft with curiosity, always looking for the winning edge. It means identifying mistakes quickly and correcting them before they compound. And it means no minor detail is too small for your attention. Excellence is built in quiet rooms, long before it shows up on a scoreboard.

Bill believed in his own Standard of Performance. He attempted to model it every day as the head coach, but real success didn't come until his players embodied that standard and expected it from each other. The foundation of a championship team was a veteran leader teaching a talented rookie to "bring your own pencil."

> *"Champions behave like champions before they're champions; they have a winning standard of performance before they are winners."*
>
> - **BILL WALSH**

Learning to win is hard work. There is no shortcut to excellence. Excellence in any endeavor demands long stretches of time and focused intensity. It requires unshakable belief, supported by consistent action.

By showing up to every meeting with a stack of notebooks and a pile of pencils, Hacksaw was passing winning habits along to his young teammates. He wasn't just preparing himself; he was teaching everyone else what preparation looked like.

You can't settle for average when you've seen the path to excellence. This book is about that path. It's about the standards that separate good from great, and the small, often unseen choices that compound into sustained success. Bill didn't build champions by chasing outcomes. He built them by defining clear standards, demanding ownership, and obsessing over preparation far before results appeared.

The stories that follow span football, business, war, exploration, and creativity. Different arenas. Same principles. Excellence is never accidental. It's earned through discipline, repetition, and the courage to do the work when no one is watching.

Never forget to bring your own pencil.

A Note to the Reader

While many coaches preferred the formality of being called "Coach," Bill Walsh insisted everyone simply call him "Bill." It wasn't casual familiarity, it was cultural intent. Bill believed the best ideas could come from anywhere, and hierarchy should never silence insight. Titles mattered less than contribution.

Throughout this book, all individuals will be referred to by their last names (or nicknames) after they are first introduced, except for Bill. Out of respect for who he was and what he stood for, we'll simply call him Bill. That's how he wanted it. And it reflects the culture he built.

While it's not the primary focus of this book, one of the things Bill was best known for was his "Standard of Performance." He clearly defined 17 points that epitomized success. Principles such as, *"Be deeply committed to learning and teaching," "Demonstrate character,"* and *"Deal appropriately with victory and defeat."* The full list is available on page 179.

These standards represent the inputs required to achieve the desired outputs. By committing to discipline, preparation, and consistent improvement, Bill believed leaders could focus entirely on what they could control. As he often said, when you follow a standard of performance, *"the score will take care of itself."* Because this philosophy formed the foundation of Bill's success, it's an important lens to keep in mind as you read the chapters that follow.

Just as great leaders must move fluidly between strategy and execution, this book intentionally alternates between the big picture and the smallest details. We begin with specific stories – often ordinary moments that reveal extraordinary standards – and then zoom out to examine the underlying principles that drove success, both for Bill and leaders in other fields.

Zoom in to study the brushstrokes. Zoom out to understand the painting.

Structurally, this book is organized into three sections, each containing three chapters. Each chapter is designed to stand on its own, allowing you to open the book anywhere and find a lesson that meets the moment. At the same time, the chapters are intentionally sequenced. Read together, they build on one another to tell a larger story.

Every chapter also follows the same rhythm. We start with a story from outside football that brings one of Bill's principles to life. We then explore how Bill embodied that principle throughout his career and in building the San Francisco 49ers. Each chapter closes with a story from another field, reinforcing how these ideas transcend any one industry.

Within every story, you'll move between the granular and the universal. Between what happened and why it mattered. That tension is intentional. Excellence lives in both places: the big picture and the small details.

Read this book the same way great leaders operate: attentive to details, anchored in principles, and always willing to zoom in or out when the moment demands it.

CARVE OUT

Military Radios

The U.S. military commonly uses two types of radios to communicate: very high frequency (VHF) and high frequency (HF). Each has distinct strengths and use cases.

A VHF radio requires "line of sight" to complete a transmission. If a hill, building, or ridgeline stands between the sender and receiver, the transmission can fail. To communicate effectively, the sender must climb to higher ground. VHF is simple but its range is limited.

An HF radio works differently. It transmits oscillating waves that bounce between the earth's surface and the ionosphere, allowing communication across vast distances. That range, however, requires more precise tuning of the equipment, certain atmospheric conditions, and some expertise from the user. When used properly, an HF radio connects exponentially farther than a VHF ever could.

The most effective leaders are like an HF radio. They can oscillate between the high-level, strategic view and the ground truth of execution – getting their hands dirty in the gritty details. It requires more expertise and deliberate tuning, but it allows teams to go much further.

CHAPTER 1

Permanent Base Camp

"You cannot stay on the summit forever; you have to come down again. So why bother in the first place? Just this: what is above knows what is below, but what is below does not know what is above. One climbs, one sees. One descends, one sees no longer, but one has seen. There is an art of conducting oneself in the lower regions by the memory of what one saw higher up. When one can no longer see, one can at least still know."

- RENÉ DAUMAL

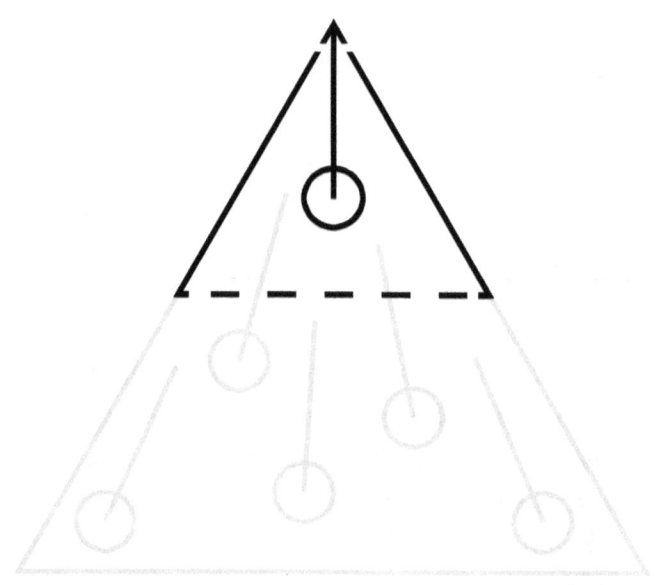

STAY WITHIN STRIKING DISTANCE
OF THE SUMMIT

Attempting to summit Mount Everest is one of the most iconic endeavors of the modern age. From the moment you land in Kathmandu, the capital of Nepal, to the moment you return home, roughly 45 days will have passed. Ascent and descent. Climbing and re-climbing. Intermittent bouts of extreme effort and agonizing boredom will define the journey. Your body strains as it attempts to acclimate to the elevation. No amount of training and no level of fitness can prepare your lungs for the Death Zone, where the majority of fatalities occur as climbers succumb to exhaustion, frostbite, and altitude sickness. On summit day (around day 32), you wake up at midnight to begin the final push, hauling oxygen tanks because there is barely enough air to breathe at 29,032 feet.

Everest Base Camp is considered the starting point for the summit attempt. It sits at 17,598 feet above sea level. For reference, the highest peak in the Lower 48 is Mount Whitney in the Sierra Nevadas of California, which stands at 14,505 feet. Base Camp, the *starting line* for Everest, is more than 3,000 feet higher. Just reaching it is an impressive physical feat. But from there, another 12,000 treacherous feet still stand between you and the summit.

When Bill Walsh was building the San Francisco 49ers from the laughingstock of professional football into a dynasty, he envisioned something similar. He believed greatness wasn't achieved by sprinting for the summit once, but by building an organization so disciplined and consistent that it could live near the top, always within reach of a championship. He called it a "Permanent Base Camp."

"I envisioned [our standards]," Bill said, "as enabling us to establish a near-permanent 'base camp' near the summit, consistently close to the top, within striking distance, never falling to the bottom of the mountain and having to start all over."

It's brutally hard to climb the mountain all over again. History is littered with one-time champions and one-hit wonders. Sustained success requires reinvention. Bill said, "You have to constantly make changes. You don't want routine practices. You don't want players to get in a comfort zone and become complacent, because that's when you start losing."

> **"Complacency creates a blatant disregard for doing what's right."**
> **- NICK SABAN**

Bill believed that standards started with the most minute details. How the receptionist answered the phone, how players tucked in their shirttails, and how coaches perfectly measured the yardage on every play diagram. The degree to which he obsessed over every detail was painstaking, but the results were undeniable.

It echoed the philosophy of UCLA's legendary basketball coach, John Wooden. On the first day of practice, he didn't talk about winning. He taught his players how to put on their socks and lace their shoes. Healthy feet alone may not win you a championship, but a bad enough blister could cost you a game.

The summit may be the vision, but you have to reach basecamp first. It's the mundane, everyday habits that get you there. Through ordinary days executed with extraordinary discipline. Before you ever breathe the thinner air of excellence near the summit, you must first hike the 40+ miles from the Lukla Airstrip to Everest Base Camp.

Los Angeles Rams coach Sean McVay asks, *"Are the habits you have for today on par with the dreams you have for tomorrow?"* Dreams don't pay the bills. Habits do. Your daily choices are the 40-mile march to basecamp – the foundation that makes sustained success possible. Put one foot in front of the other. Keep going.

Establishing a permanent base camp that keeps your team within striking distance of championship-level success begins with people. Those who can commit to the standard and uphold it even in the most challenging of circumstances. Whether you're building a team to compete for a Super Bowl or scale Mount Everest, it's essential to assemble people who know the terrain.

Sherpa guides are masters of navigating the Everest trek. Without their expertise, danger and certain failure lurk around every corner. As Philadelphia Eagles coach Nick Sirianni says, "You can't be great without the greatness of others." The more difficult the journey, the more specific the skillset required for success. As a leader, you can't do it all. You need to find people who are masters of their craft. The art of leadership is molding these unique skillsets and egos into a team. When done right, the whole becomes far greater than the sum of its parts.

For the ones that make it, the average amount of time at the summit of Everest is fifteen to twenty minutes. Sometimes as little as five minutes, depending on oxygen supply. Why would someone dedicate years of preparation, sacrifice, and suffering for such a brief moment?

Ask high achievers and peak performers, and you'll hear the same answer: the work is the reward. The journey, the striving, the pursuit is what gives them purpose. The daily commitment to something difficult and worthwhile. They establish permanent basecamps in their lives so they are always within striking distance of an audacious goal. Trophies gather dust, but the pursuit of excellence reveals character and defines your life.

You can't live at the summit. There simply isn't enough air. The day after you win a championship or close a deal, you're back in line competing once again.

There is no mystery to mastery. Only focus and consistency sustained over time. The best time to start your march to Basecamp is now.

Section One

The Path

CARVE OUT

Into the Storm

A storm is coming. The temperature drops, rain and hail pelt the ground, and gale-force winds tear across the landscape. All animals turn and run, instinctively fleeing the danger.

Except the bison.

While others scatter in search of safety, bison turn toward the storm and charge directly into it. They don't try to outrun it. They push straight through the center, accelerating toward the other side.

Animals that run end up prolonging their exposure, trapped beneath the storm as it overtakes them. The bison, by facing it head-on, minimize their time in the harshest conditions. The fastest way out is through.

If the storm is inevitable, don't run from it. Turn and face it. Oftentimes, the only way forward is straight through.

CHAPTER 2

Self-Belief Before Evidence

"Many of life's failures are people who did not realize how close they were to success when they gave up."

- THOMAS EDISON

"Success is the ability to go from one failure to another with no loss of enthusiasm."

- WINSTON CHURCHILL

PERSEVERE UNTIL
YOU MAKE IT

The name "Dyson" now sits in millions of homes, synonymous with innovation and design. But for more than a decade, James Dyson was buried in debt, rejected by nearly every major manufacturer in his industry, and building prototype after prototype in near anonymity. Before experiencing any semblance of success, doubt, risk, and uncertainty defined his life.

When Dyson began his journey, the vacuum cleaner market was dominated by one company: Hoover. Their primary design hadn't meaningfully changed in nearly a century, and few believed it ever would. If a better vacuum existed, conventional wisdom said Hoover would have built it already.

Dyson didn't begin as a vacuum cleaner revolutionary, though. He began as a designer. Curious, stubborn, and undeterred by convention, he learned early that progress comes not from theory, but from action. Early in his career, he worked under the inventive engineer, Jeremy Fry, who believed deeply in learning by doing. Fry didn't ask whether something could be done. He simply expected you to try. That attitude shaped Dyson. As Fry liked to say, "You don't think about something, you just do it."

After seven years of working with Fry, Dyson decided to build something of his own. His first major invention was the Ballbarrow, a redesigned wheelbarrow with a large rotating ball instead of a front wheel. Since traditional wheelbarrows sank and tipped, it solved a real problem. But Dyson quickly learned a tough lesson: even great products fail if the opportunity is too small. Despite capturing much of the market, the company never became meaningfully profitable.

There just weren't enough people who needed a wheelbarrow, and the margins were too tight.

Though the Ballbarrow failed financially, it trained him for what came next. He learned about pricing, market size, and ownership. About how craftsmanship alone isn't always enough. But it planted the seed for his next invention. And *how you finish one chapter determines how you begin the next.*

> ### *I have not failed. I've just found 10,000 ways that won't work.*
>
> **- THOMAS EDISON**

Dyson's true breakthrough came in an unexpected place: the paint booth. While painting the frames for the Ballbarrows, Dyson noticed how inefficient the powder-coating vacuum systems were. Asking around, he learned that sawmills used cyclones – spinning chambers that separated dust without clogging. Curious, he snuck into a nearby mill one night by scaling the wall, took measurements, and replicated the design. Soon after, he built a 30-foot cyclone for his Ballbarrow factory. Seeing that it worked so efficiently, he had an idea.

Rushing home one day in 1978, Dyson built a small cyclone prototype out of cardboard and Scotch tape, attached it to his Hoover vacuum with a piece of hose, and watched as it worked. Where traditional vacuums lost suction as their bags filled, the cyclone never clogged. Dyson knew he was onto something.

Investors, however, didn't see things the same way. If

this idea was truly better, they argued, Hoover would have already built it. That logic didn't stop Dyson, but it did leave him with few supporters and no money. Without any major backers, he returned to his original mentor, Fry, raised partial funding, took out loans, and retreated to his backyard shed. There, he began what would later become legend.

Newly married and experimenting with ideas, Dyson and his wife quietly accumulated enormous debt. By the time it was paid off when he was 48 years old, it totaled almost a million dollars in today's terms. He had no safety net and no guarantee of payoff. Just years of uncertainty while chasing something he believed should exist, even if the world thought it a waste of time.

Over the course of about five years, Dyson built and tested 5,127 prototypes, changing one variable at a time. No computer simulations or shortcuts. Just relentless iteration. Failure after failure, each one taught him something new.

Joseph Campbell once wrote, "If the path before you is clear, you're probably on someone else's."

Dyson's path was anything but clear. After years of rejection, a small Japanese company agreed to license his design. The deal was modest, but it gave him enough runway to keep building. Through the brief partnership, Dyson decided he wanted full control of his product and eventually bet everything. He took out a £600,000 loan, put his house up as collateral, and began manufacturing vacuums himself.

After 13 long years, success finally arrived. By the mid 1990s, the Dyson was the best-selling vacuum in the UK, generating roughly $100 million in revenue. Within a few years, one in four British households owned one. What many called an "overnight success" was, in reality, the product of decades of doubt, debt, and thousands of failed attempts.

"Despite all the setbacks, the lawsuits, the cash crises, the ridicule, the bad feelings, and the doubt," Dyson later said, "I always knew deep down."

He had *self belief before evidence.* Those who persevere the longest don't avoid failure, they accumulate it. They endure rejection and uncertainty not because they are immune to it, but because something inside them refuses to stop. Perseverance isn't blind stubbornness, it's commitment to a standard when results haven't arrived yet. It's a willingness to learn, adjust, and iterate without giving up.

> *When you feel like giving up, it's precisely the point when everyone else gives up. It's at that point that you must put in extra effort. You do that, and then success is right around the corner.*
>
> **- JAMES DYSON**

Those who succeed the most also have the most failures. They are the ones who, despite how many times they fall, get back up and try again, until the world finally catches up to what they believed all along.

▼

Winners Act Like Winners Before They Are Winners

In 2005, Paul Graham founded Y Combinator, the startup accelerator that would go on to launch companies like Airbnb, Dropbox, Reddit, and Stripe. Graham later explained that when interviewing programmers, the single most important thing he looked for was what they worked on in their spare time.

"You can't do anything really well unless you love it," Graham said. "And if you love to hack, you'll inevitably be working on projects of your own."

Interest isn't enough. To win big, you have to be obsessed.

Bill Walsh understood that instinctively. Long before championships, fame, or job titles, football wasn't only his *job;* it was something he studied. He often spoke about passion not as motivation, but as devotion to the craft itself. "Passion," Bill said, "is a love for the act of teaching – believing in your heart that it is not a means to an end, but an end in itself." It's easy to see Bill's passion years later, calling plays on the sideline of the NFC Championship Game in Candlestick Park. But the truest evidence appears well before his professional success.

> ### *Champions behave like champions before they are champions*
> - BILL WALSH

To understand Bill, you need to know that he was the "new kid." Because of his father's job, he moved from Los

Angeles to Oregon to San Francisco. He attended three high schools in three years as his family traveled up and down the Pacific Coast. "Having to be the new kid always destroyed me," Bill later said, "but without football I would have been lost."

Football became his constant. Each summer, training camp was his proving ground, not just athletically, but socially. Football helped Bill acclimate to his new environment when everything else was uncertain.

He went on to play for a young coach named Bob Bronzan at San Jose State. At only 33 years old when Bill enrolled, Bronzan was an innovator and an educator. Bill described him as "A [football] theorist and excellent teacher… he coached football like it was a science, a skilled sport instead of just head bashing." Bronzan's approach had a lasting impact on Bill and his fellow teammates. The influence was so profound that nearly a third of that San Jose State roster would later go into coaching.

When Bill finished his playing career, he stayed on as a graduate assistant under Bronzan while earning his master's degree in physical education. Instead of choosing a safe or conventional thesis topic, Bill convinced the faculty to allow him to write a thesis titled: Flank Formation Football – Stress: Defense.

His thesis sketched out the history of offensive football, allowing Bill to explain where he thought the game was going. It was an early blueprint. Though unfinished and imperfect, it's clear he was beginning to build the foundation of what would one day become the West Coast Offense. There were many things Bill could have written to fulfill the requirements of his master's program. He chose to write over

200 pages on how to stress opposing defenses.

Historian David McCullough famously said, "Writing is thinking. To write well is to think clearly. That's why it's so hard."

Bill is an incredible example of Paul Graham's interview question: What do you write in your spare time? The obsession he demonstrated for the game was evident early. Writing is thinking, and as a young coach, Bill was thinking about offensive football…a lot.

It's not enough to think. Eventually, you have to apply your theories. You need to back your belief with action.

In 1957, Bill was hired as the head coach at Washington Union High School in the East Bay of California. The program had lost 26 of its previous 27 games. For Bill, it was a blank canvas. And he experimented relentlessly.

He changed his offense three times during his first season. Ideas were tested, discarded, refined, and rebuilt as he iterated on what he called "the Walsh offense," a synthesis of everything he'd been collecting across his football life. What began as experimentation was forming the foundation for his life's work.

"In those days," Bill said, "almost all football coaches were afraid of the passing game. People thought it made you weak, that you couldn't have a tough team if you passed too much." He was determined to change the way the game was played. Football wasn't just a test of physical toughness, it could be an artistic expression. Bill studied obsessively. He attended coaching clinics and practiced interviewing for jobs alone in his office with chalk in hand. His preparation built confidence long before results validated it.

As Bronzan later said, "I knew if he got to the blackboard, he had the job."

Self-belief comes before evidence.

That belief wasn't loud or performative. It was built quietly, through work done in isolation. In empty rooms, in front of blank chalkboards, and during long nights refining ideas no one had yet endorsed.

Is your drive dependent on outside recognition, or is it sustained by internal conviction?

What are you willing to work on in the shadows?

Are you willing to confront an empty blackboard with nothing more than chalk and everything you've learned?

It is crucial for coaches to encourage obsession. As a leader, it always starts with you. Following your own obsession will allow your full authenticity to show. You can't fake it.

It was Bill's number one rule for leaders: "Be yourself. I am not Vince Lombardi; Vince Lombardi was not Bill Walsh. My style was my style, and it worked for me. Your style will work for you when you take advantage of your strengths and strive to overcome your weaknesses. You must be the best version of yourself you can be; stay within the framework of your own personality and be authentic. If you're faking it, you'll be found out."

Start by living your own obsession authentically. Then invite others to do the same.

In *The Hitchhiker's Guide to the Galaxy*, Douglas Adams wrote, "We can't win against obsession. They care, we don't. They win." Over time, obsession simply outpaces interest, talent, and convenience.

Bill lived that truth before anyone knew his name.

Though he wasn't the most gifted athlete on the field, football was a constant in his life. Through the ups and downs, the game anchored his identity. As his vision focused, his aspirations grew.

From high school coach to Super Bowl Champion was a long, winding road. Between 1957 and 1979, Bill coached receivers, defensive backs, and running backs. He painted practice fields and called the offensive plays. He worked for run-down, semi-professional leagues and at elite academic institutions. He endured long stretches without validation, promotion, or certainty that his ideas would ever matter. What sustained him was not confidence based on results, but the discipline to keep refining his standards before the world rewarded them.

By doing the work, the evidence accrues and compounds. Self-belief gets you started. It's what fuels the work. It is the internal force that keeps you going even when the outside world hasn't recognized your growth. Then discipline keeps you moving. Ultimately, your confidence can only come from doing the work. Some may find quick paths to outside recognition, but there are no shortcuts to inner excellence.

You have to do the work. You have to persevere until you make it.

▼

Conviction is Contagious

Growing up in Florida, Sara Blakely wanted to become a lawyer. But after failing the Law School Admission Test

(LSAT) twice, that dream seemed out of reach. After college, she faced another rejection when she failed her audition for the part of Goofy at Disney World, settling for a job as a ride greeter instead. Then, in the early 1990s, she eventually landed a job selling fax machines door-to-door. Far from glamorous work, it came with slammed doors, awkward conversations, and her business card being ripped up in front of her face. Yet, the daily exposure to rejection resulted in something else: preparation.

Failure didn't intimidate Blakely the way it did most people. Growing up, her father reframed failure as something to be proud of. Each night at dinner, he asked his children what they had failed at that day. If they had tried something and failed, he celebrated it. Blakely later reflected that this ritual permanently rewired how she viewed failure, "Failure for me became not trying, versus the outcome." That mindset stayed with her.

While selling fax machines, Blakely was often wearing hosiery as part of her business attire, and found that none of the existing options felt right or looked good under clothing. So she started experimenting. One day, she cut the feet off a pair of control-top pantyhose to improve how her clothes fit and looked. It was make-shift, but it worked.

She knew two things almost immediately. First, there had to be a better solution. And second, she couldn't be the only woman with this problem. Plus, after seven years of selling fax machines, she was desperate for something bigger.

Before quitting her job or spending real money, Blakely decided to test her idea. She visited craft stores to experiment with fabrics. She sifted through existing patents to see if anything like her idea already existed. Finding none, she then walked into a local Neiman Marcus and asked a sales associate a simple question: would women buy footless pantyhose to wear under pants? The associate told her customers had been asking for exactly that, and some had even tried making their own versions. That was enough.

In 1998, without any experience in fashion or manufacturing, and without ever having taken a business class, Blakely invested her savings of $5,000 to develop a prototype. Thus, Spanx was born. She continued selling fax machines to pay the bills and keep her health insurance, but worked nights and weekends on designs and cold-calling manufacturers.

When those calls went nowhere, Blakely stepped it up a notch. Taking a week off of work, she went to North Carolina to show up in person at all the mills she had been trying to call. What she encountered was skepticism, confusion, and an industry that hadn't changed in decades. Ironically, almost all of the people she met with were men, and they didn't understand her product, much less the problem it solved. After dozens of meetings and countless no's, nothing happened. Until a few weeks later, her phone rang.

One of the mill owners in Charlotte called her back. After meeting with Blakely earlier, he had gone home and mentioned the idea at dinner. He had three daughters who immediately understood and urged him to give it a chance. He later admitted he still didn't fully get the idea, but Blakely's conviction had stuck with him. After months of rejection, she finally had her first yes.

Conviction is contagious. Believing, when grounded in effort and clarity, compels others to believe alongside you.

Her next obstacle was protecting the idea. Unable to find a single female patent attorney in the state of Georgia at the time, Blakely tried explaining the product to several male attorneys. None were impressed, and each quoted her between $3,000 and $5,000; money she didn't have. So she did what she'd done all along. She figured it out herself.

Blakely went to Barnes & Noble, bought a book on patents and trademarks, and wrote the patent application on her own. Her mother, an artist, sketched the prototype. Blakely then returned to the attorney who had been most helpful, handed him the nearly complete work, and asked him to help finalize the claims for a reduced fee. He agreed, clearing yet another roadblock.

With product in hand, Blakely became her own marketing department. In 2000, she set her sights on Neiman Marcus. Looking up their number in the Yellow Pages, she called the local Atlanta office and was laughed at. On the call, she learned the buying office was in Dallas, so she called there instead. And she kept calling for several days, at different times of the day, until she finally reached the hosiery buyer. After pleading for just ten minutes of the buyer's time, she was granted a meeting. Given the green light, Blakely flew to Dallas with her prototype in a Ziploc bag and her lucky red college backpack.

Midway through her pitch to the buyer, she could tell things weren't going well. So she took a risk. Pausing the meeting, she asked the lady to come to the bathroom with her. There, she changed into her product and showed it in real time. Seeing it in use, the buyer was immediately sold on the idea, and Neiman Marcus agreed to place Spanx in seven stores as a trial.

For Blakely, the real work had just begun. She paid friends to buy the product and spread the word. She stood in stores all day, open to close, demonstrating Spanx to customers. She ran morning rallies for sales associates, offering incentives, free products, and contests to motivate them to sell. With limited rack space, she knew traction was everything for Neiman Marcus to even consider a second order.

By watching customers, she learned another critical lesson: her buyers weren't shopping in the hosiery section. They were looking in shoes and ready-to-wear. So she bought her own display stands and placed Spanx next to cash registers throughout Neiman Marcus. Without any approval, her confidence led employees to assume someone else, higher up, had approved it.

At the same time, she continued shipping orders from her apartment. One of those orders eventually got to Oprah. Oprah's hairdresser received it, placed it in her dressing room, and Oprah immediately fell in love. Spanx was named the product of the year. From there, the momentum was unstoppable.

Spanx soon landed in Saks Fifth Avenue and Bloomingdale's. By 2012, Blakely became the youngest self-made female billionaire, according to Forbes.

Blakely often says the real reward wasn't financial. It was discovering who she became through the process.

Perseverance isn't loud. It's patient. It's the quiet willingness to keep showing up; refining, testing, and believing without any guarantees. Those who persevere until they make it don't avoid failure. They commit to a standard, believe in themselves, and trust the results will eventually follow.

CHAPTER 3

The Valley of Death

"*The cave you fear to enter holds the treasure you seek.*"

\- JOSEPH CAMPBELL

"*Take care of the minutes; the hours will take care of themselves.*"

-PHILIP DORMER STANHOPE,
The 4th Earl of Chesterfield

"*Pain is inevitable. Suffering is optional.*"

-KEVIN KELLY

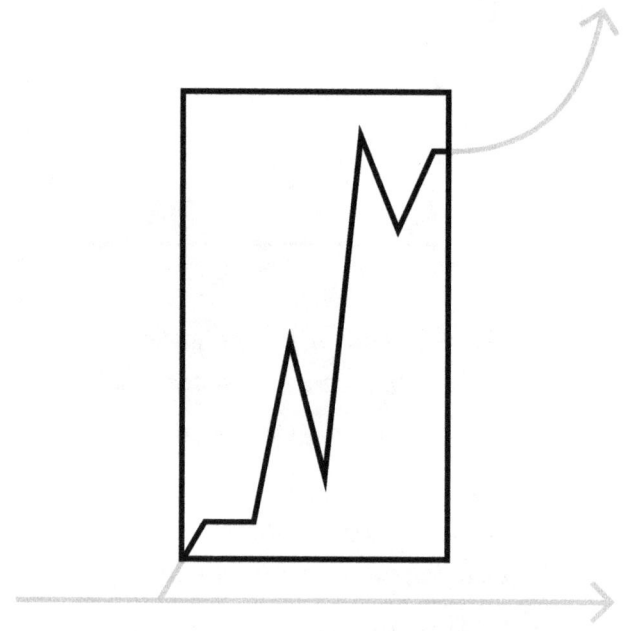

THE ONLY WAY IS THROUGH

In the early 1960s, the global running shoe market was dominated by established brands like Adidas and Puma. Few outsiders had the capital or credibility to challenge them. The idea that an American startup could compete with the German giants was, to most people, laughable.

But in one of his final Stanford Business School classes, Phil Knight wrote a paper arguing that Japanese running shoes could disrupt the market just as Japanese cameras had previously disrupted the German incumbents. As a lifelong runner who had trained under famed Oregon track coach Bill Bowerman, the idea was deeply personal to Knight, and he just couldn't let it go. It felt crazy, but also inevitable. He devoured every book on importing and exporting he could find. The concept didn't just interest him, it consumed him.

After graduating in 1962, Knight embarked on a trip around the world with one specific stop in mind: Japan. He had no company, no plan, and no experience; just a conviction that wouldn't let him go.

Following a long detour in Hawaii, he finally arrived in Kobe, a major port city in southern Japan, and somehow landed a meeting with Onitsuka (now ASICS), the makers of Tiger running shoes. Despite showing up at the wrong building, sprinting across town, and arriving 45 minutes late, Knight delivered a pitch bold enough to earn him the exclusive distribution rights in the western part of the U.S.

The Onitsuka executives weren't aware that Knight didn't actually have a company, and when they asked the name of his firm, he improvised. Thinking back to the track ribbons hanging in his childhood bedroom, he blurted out the first thing that came to mind: Blue Ribbon Sports.

> *"Let everyone else call your idea crazy. Just keep going. Don't stop. Don't even think about stopping until you get there. Whatever comes, just don't stop."*
>
> - **PHIL KNIGHT**

Over a year after that meeting in Japan, the first shipment of shoes finally arrived. Knight mailed two pairs to his revered coach, Bowerman. Bowerman instantly saw potential; not just in the shoes, but in Knight. He proposed a partnership. Bowerman would obsess over design, while Knight would handle sales and finance. Together, they formally launched Blue Ribbon Sports in 1964.

Bowerman was relentless in his quest to shave ounces off a shoe, famously noting that one ounce removed from a shoe saves a runner 55 pounds over a mile. *Ounces equal pounds.* Small things compound. Bowerman's mindset would become the spiritual blueprint for Nike. A contrarian in every sense, he despised being called "Coach." He considered himself a teacher first, calling himself a "professor of competitive responses." He preached rest and recovery decades before sports science caught up. And he obsessed over details others ignored. All of it shaped Knight.

Meanwhile, Knight worked out of his parents' basement, fighting to keep the business alive one shipment at a time. He held a full-time accounting job at Price Waterhouse to pay the bills, which he hated, but it afforded him unique exposure to how other companies worked. Living on the edge of default every month, banks told him to quit, and his father ridiculed him for "messing around with shoes" instead of focusing on a real job. Sporting goods stores refused to carry his shoes because "the world doesn't need another track shoe."

Aside from Bowerman, it seemed the entire world was pushing against Knight's success. Everyone, except his mom. One evening, she overheard Knight's dad scolding him for continuing to pursue the shoe business. Boldly stepping into the kitchen, she reached into her purse, pulled out $7, and told Knight that she would like to buy a pair. She then regularly wore them around the house, proudly displaying her size six Japanese running shoes. When you're fighting to survive, it's those little moments of belief that propel you forward.

Knight began driving all over the Pacific Northwest, selling shoes out of the trunk of his Plymouth Valiant at local track meets. Between races, he would chat with every coach, runner, or fan who would give him the time of day. And suddenly, the demand was undeniable. He couldn't write orders fast enough. Having previously sold encyclopedias, and later mutual funds while on his trip around the world, Knight had grown to despise the act of "selling." But everything was different with these shoes. He found that he wasn't selling, he was simply expressing his own belief, and he quickly found that people wanted some of that belief for themselves. Conviction is contagious.

> *"The best thing about startups is you only ever experience two emotions: euphoria and terror."*
>
> - MARC ANDREESSEN

But belief did not insulate him from setbacks. Soon, another U.S. distributor for Onitsuka sent a cease-and-desist letter. Shipments arrived late. Payments were delayed and the banks tightened credit. Knight constantly felt like he was building on top of sand. Just when he'd get traction, the ground shifted beneath him. He lived in what entrepreneurs call the "Valley of Death," the phase where the dream feels impossible and the temptation to quit is overwhelming.

He worked insane hours, without any semblance of a social life or sense of personal care. He slept in his office to save money. And yet, he felt more alive than ever because he was chasing something that felt like a calling. When you find what you love to do, no one can keep up.

> *"Find what feels like play to you but looks like work to others."*
>
> **- NAVAL RAVIKANT**

Still, the walls kept closing in. Knight personally guaranteed loans and put nearly everything he owned at risk.

After seven years, the company moved to terminate their contract altogether. Knight was on the brink of losing all he had built. In a moment of desperation during a meeting, he stole a document from an Onitsuka rep's briefcase and discovered a list of appointments with other potential distributors, confirming that Onitsuka planned to cut him out.

When the partnership finally collapsed in 1971, Knight fought back in court and won. Blue Ribbon would survive, but now without a supplier. The only option was to become their own.

Through the valley of death, Nike was born.

A Portland State student designed the iconic Swoosh logo for $35. The first line of Nike shoes debuted at the 1972 Olympic Trials with Steve Prefontaine as the brand's rebel ambassador. For Knight, Prefontaine wasn't just an athlete, he embodied Nike's soul: grit, defiance, and relentless forward motion. "It's not about the shoes, it's about what you do in the shoes."

Even as Nike grew, survival was never guaranteed. Knight maxed out every credit card, living deal to deal. He constantly feared losing everything. As he later wrote, "The art of competing is the art of forgetting. You must forget your limits, your doubts, your pain, your past. You must forget that internal voice screaming, begging, 'not one more step,' and when you can't forget it, you must negotiate with it."

In December 1980, nearly twenty years after that first moonshot meeting in Japan, Nike went public. The man who once sold shoes from the trunk of his car was suddenly worth hundreds of millions of dollars. But for Knight, the Initial Public Offering (IPO) was more closure than triumph. He had managed to climb out of the valley of death.

Looking back, Knight had one piece of advice he wished he'd understood earlier: don't settle for a job or even a career. Seek a calling. Even if you don't know what that means, seek it. If you're following a calling, the fatigue will be easier to bear, the disappointments will be fewer, and the highs will be unlike anything you've ever felt. And perhaps his most important lesson: "Don't ever stop."

> *"One day, in retrospect,*
> *the years of struggle will strike*
> *you as the most beautiful."*
>
> - SIGMUND FREUD

Those chasing comfort never make it out of the valley of death. Only those chasing a calling live to see the other side. The valley is part of every meaningful endeavor. And *success often emerges just beyond the point where most would give up.*

▼

The Valley of Death in San Francisco

A "false start" penalty costs an offense five yards. Over the course of a football game, where teams routinely rack up hundreds of yards, it shouldn't matter that much, right? But to Bill Walsh, a false start penalty was the ultimate breakdown in discipline. It meant a player had allowed frustration with the past or concern for the future to cloud their mind. A split-second lack of focus caused them to forget the most fundamental starting point of a football play – the snap count. It was a reminder that success, especially under pressure, comes down to focus on what you can control *right now*.

Bill experienced his own false starts throughout his career. When disappointment hit, he returned to fundamentals. Don't dwell on the past or get lost in the future. Stay in the moment and control what's controllable.

Bill famously said, "Concentrate on what will produce

results rather than on the results, focus on the process, not the prize." But even for someone as disciplined and process-oriented as Bill, the temptation to chase outcomes was ever-present.

If there was one thing Bill wanted more than anything, it was to be a head coach in the National Football League. From the time he wrote his master's thesis at San Jose State through his rise as the offensive coordinator of the Cincinnati Bengals, he was preparing for that opportunity. Working and studying under the legendary Paul Brown, Bill believed he was being groomed as the natural successor.

When the moment came, Brown passed over his young offensive coordinator, instead giving the job to longtime offensive line coach Bill "Tiger" Johnson. The move was devastating to Bill and felt deeply personal. Just as Bill was nearing the summit of his professional life, the storms of uncertainty rushed in. He would have to find a new route to his goal.

Disoriented and in search of another opportunity, Bill left the Bengals to be the offensive coordinator for the San Diego Chargers, and after one season, became the head coach at Stanford University. One rung at a time, he kept climbing the coaching ladder. Still, an NFL head coaching opportunity felt just out of reach. After two impressive seasons at Stanford, the call finally came: the San Francisco 49ers. Unfortunately, they were unquestionably the worst franchise in the NFL.

The job offer came from Eddie DeBartolo Jr., the eccentric son of a real estate magnate from Youngstown, Ohio. Having led Stanford to back-to-back bowl games, Bill and his team were set to take on the University of Georgia in the Bluebonnet Bowl. Excited to watch his future coach in action, DeBartolo Jr. gathered a large group of friends and acquaintances at his Youngstown mansion.

Unfortunately, what he saw was a disaster. The "offensive genius" whom he had just hired in San Francisco looked anything but that, as Georgia jumped out to an early 15-0 lead by the end of the first half. To make matters worse, the Bulldogs took the opening drive of the second half straight down the field for another touchdown.

On the Stanford sideline, Bill paced, wondering if his dream of being an NFL head coach was unraveling before it began. Bill imagined DeBartolo Jr. sitting with all of his friends, expecting a coronation (or at the very least a competitive game). Instead, Stanford was being blown off the field.

But Bill's superpower was his ability to adjust. He learned from Bob Bronzan to practice the game of football situationally and account for every contingency. When an opponent threw a punch, Bill always had a counterpunch tucked away.

Georgia's blitz was overwhelming Stanford's pass protection. Quarterback Steve Dils was missing the deep out-breaking routes because his offensive line couldn't hold up against the rush. So, Bill countered by throwing the ball "hot" – quick passes into the space vacated by the blitz.

The strategy worked to perfection, and Stanford stormed back. One drive at a time, they chipped away, eventually taking the lead 25-22 in the 4th quarter. They hung on to win, and as time expired, Dils took the final snap and dove to the ground in celebration. When the final whistle blew,

Bill knew his dream was finally a reality.

He made it. At 47 years old, Bill had achieved his goal of becoming an NFL head coach. But it was a false summit. There was much more work to be done to transform the 49ers from the doormat of the NFL to a competitive team and, eventually, a champion. Bill had a long road ahead, and the real climb was just beginning.

After a dismal two-win first season in San Francisco, year two appeared more promising. With the off-season to address roster concerns and further install his system of offense, Bill's young 49ers appeared to take to the changes quickly. They rattled off three straight wins to start the 1980 season, already surpassing the previous year's win total. Bill was feeling confident when suddenly the season took a turn for the worse. They proceeded to lose seven straight games, and all of their early momentum evaporated.

Heading into their matchup against Hall of Fame coach Don Shula's high-powered Miami Dolphins, Bill was desperate to get back in the win column and stop the bleeding.

Bill carried his anxiety into the game. He later admitted he was "out of character – I was brusque, short-tempered, and not as tuned in as I should have been."

Despite the odds stacked against them, the 49ers battled late into the 4th quarter. Kicker Ray Wersching nailed a 47-yard field goal to bring them within one point. The 49ers felt a surge of momentum, but it didn't last long. Bill looked out on the field and saw yellow flags littering the offensive backfield. The points were taken off the board as a result of a holding penalty on the play. They were forced to punt, and on the following drive, quarterback Steve DeBerg was intercepted in the red zone. The game was over. The 49ers had lost eight straight games. Bill felt the weight of the world on his shoulders and, though he felt his team was prepared and playing well, they simply couldn't catch a break. The season had spiraled out of control.

On the cross-country flight home from Florida, Bill broke down and wept. "A job I had worked for my entire adult life was in jeopardy," he said. Feeling like a failure, he prepared to resign his post and admit he didn't have what it took to be an NFL head coach.

This was the valley of death. The gut-wrenching stretch every successful person has faced at some point in their journey. When quitting feels logical and external failure triggers an internal crisis. Bill had accomplished his lifelong dream of becoming an NFL head coach, but after less than two seasons on the job, he was ready to throw in the towel. Self-belief had gotten him the job, but his growing self-doubt in the face of endless obstacles was threatening his ability to continue on.

The valley often presents itself as external circumstances and outside adversity, but the real battle is within.

Can you confront reality without surrendering belief? Can you get back to work when confidence is gone, and your back is against the wall?

The valley of death can't be avoided. It has to be met head-on. Confront the brutal facts, make the necessary changes, and get back to work. "I must stand and fight, or it was all over," Bill said. "I began pulling myself together… I was able to summon strength enough to pull my focus, my thinking, out of the past and move it forward to our next big problem."

Bill later offered this advice for anyone experiencing such a crucible: "Allow yourself the 'grieving time,' but then recognize that the road to recovery and victory lies in having the strength to get up off the mat and start planning your next move. For me, on that flight back home after the Miami loss, it meant working *one minute at a time* – literally – to regain composure, confidence, and direction."

Often, when things are at their worst, you're closer than you can imagine to success. Just sixteen months after that low point in Miami, Bill was hoisting the Lombardi Trophy as a Super Bowl Champion. Those tools forged in the valley – the discipline, resilience, and clarity – are what make success possible.

The 49ers' path to their first Super Bowl felt like an impossible climb. But as Bill understood, victory requires confronting the harsh realities without succumbing to despair. Jim Collins would later call this the Stockdale Paradox: unwavering faith in eventual success paired with the discipline to face the harsh facts of the present.

Don't run. Don't hide.

The climb always feels impossible in the moment. Face everything head-on.

The only way is through.

▼

Ernest Shackleton and the *Endurance* Expedition

In 1914, Sir Ernest Shackleton set sail with one of the boldest ambitions of the age: to be the first expedition to cross Antarctica over land. Shackleton was no novice. He was a decorated explorer, knighted by the King of England, and revered across Europe. He had come within 97 miles of the South Pole on a previous expedition and knew history was closing in. If he didn't act soon, someone else would claim the glory.

He named their ship *Endurance* after his family motto, *By endurance we conquer.* To find the right men for the grueling trip, Shackleton placed an ad that has since become legendary:

"Men wanted for hazardous journey. Small wages, bitter cold, long months of complete darkness, constant danger, safe return doubtful. Honour and recognition in case of success."

Shackleton chose speed over total preparedness. Studying past expeditions, he noticed that teams burdened by contingency plans and excess supplies fared worse than those that traveled light. So he stripped the mission to essentials. Every item had to earn its place because every ounce mattered.

About a month after departing South Georgia Island, the *Endurance* became trapped in the frozen Weddell Sea. For months, the ship drifted helplessly as the ice tightened around it. The pressure mounted until the hull began to splinter.

In October 1915, the ice finally crushed the ship. The expedition was over. Shackleton and his 27-man crew stood on drifting ice floes in subzero temperatures, hundreds of miles from civilization. There was no radio. No rescue. No planes capable of reaching them. The Southern Ocean might as well have been another planet. The only way out was to save themselves.

From that moment on, there was only one mission – *get every man home alive.* For nearly two years, the crew endured starvation, darkness, hypothermia, and constant danger as the ice beneath them cracked and shifted. Shackleton led his team into the valley of death head-on, relying on disciplined action, fundamentals, and persistence in the face of every obstacle. He was relentless about keeping the men focused on just the next step.

When fresh water ran out and food became scarce, they drank seal blood. When morale wavered, Shackleton kept the team physically and mentally occupied. Survival required a narrowing of attention until nothing existed beyond the next essential task.

> *"A mind that can maintain its lightness will not come undone in war."*
>
> **- STEVEN PRESSFIELD**

Eventually, the ice could no longer support them. Shackleton ordered the men into lifeboats and navigated through freezing seas until they reached a barren, windswept outcrop, later named Elephant Island. It was the first solid ground they had stood on in nearly 500 days, completely uninhabited and far from any shipping lanes. Shackleton confronted the brutal facts that if they stayed, they would die.

So he made an impossible choice. He left the majority of his crew on Elephant Island under the command of Frank Wild, instructing them to hold on and keep faith, no matter how long it took. Then he selected a handful of men to join him in a single 22-foot lifeboat. With no escort, no guarantee of rescue, and winter closing in, Shackleton set out across 800 miles of the Southern Ocean, through some of the most violent seas on Earth. The small crew battled towering waves, freezing spray, exhaustion, and the persistent danger of capsizing. Against all odds, they reached South Georgia Island, but landed on the wrong side.

Still not finished with the nightmare expedition, Shackleton and two of his crew then crossed the island's unmapped mountains and glaciers on foot, without tents or proper climbing equipment, completing the first-ever overland crossing of South Georgia. They reached a whaling station on May 20, 1916. And after multiple failed attempts, Shackleton returned to Elephant Island with a rescue ship to save the twenty-two castaways he had left behind. They had survived for over four long months, and every single man was still alive.

You don't escape the valley through brilliance. You escape it by endurance. By stepping into the storm instead of waiting for it to pass. By persisting when quitting feels more rational.

In the valley of death, long-term plans are useless and inspiration is unreliable. Survival depends on fundamentals, discipline, and the refusal to stop moving forward. You can't dwell on the past, nor cower in the shadow of the future. All you can do is focus on the next best step.

That's how every great journey makes it to the other side; not because the valley disappears, but because someone chooses to walk through it.

CHAPTER 4

Don't Quit A Hit Show

"Success is not final, failure is not fatal: It is the courage to continue that counts."

- **WINSTON CHURCHILL**

"The easiest thing to sell is your passion. The hardest is selling yourself when you are exhausted."

- **PHIL KNIGHT**

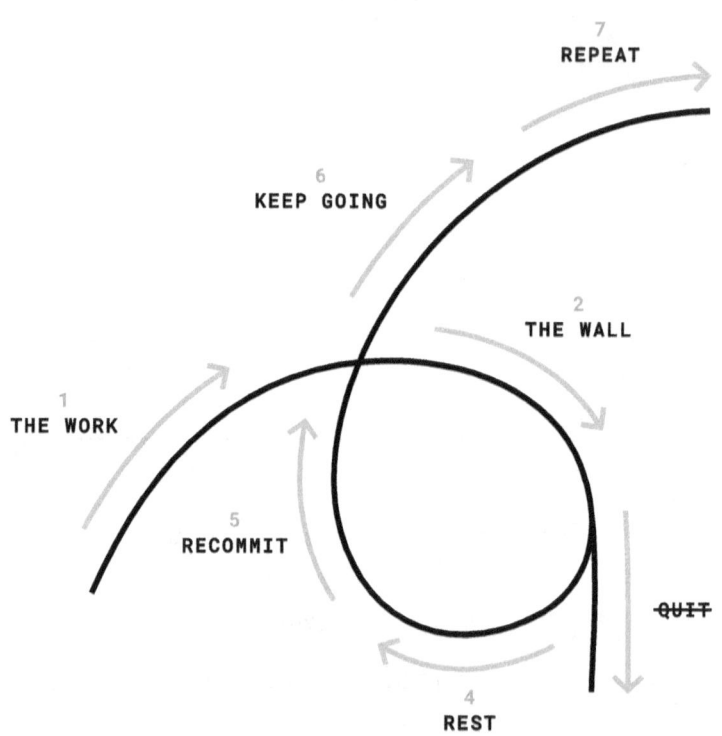

DON'T QUIT — REST AND RECOMMIT

By age 55, Theodore Roosevelt had lived more life than nearly any other figure in American history. He had charged up San Juan Hill as a Rough Rider, reformed New York politics as governor, served as Vice President, and had become the youngest President in American history. He brokered peace agreements, confronted monopolies, conserved millions of acres of public land, and redefined the modern presidency through sheer willpower and stamina.

But when Roosevelt left office in 1909, he didn't know who he was without the relentless demands of leadership. For a decade, politics had fueled him. He thrived on urgency, conflict, and a purposeful mission. So when he split from the Republican Party and lost the 1912 presidential election running as the Progressive "Bull Moose" candidate, the defeat shook him. The man who embodied boundless energy fell into deep depression; embarrassed, exhausted, and unsure of what came next.

Instead of reflecting on everything he had accomplished (described as "the gain" in Ben Hardy and Dan Sullivan's book, *The Gap and the Gain*), Roosevelt fixated on the gap between where he stood and where he believed he should be. And when high achievers stare only at the gap, the instinct is to chase the next big challenge to fill the void.

Physical exertion had always been Roosevelt's medicine. Even as a sickly child with debilitating asthma, he embodied Rich Cohen's line that "*A man can free his soul only by exhausting his body.*" When his spirit and confidence faltered, he sought difficulty. Not one to take a step back, he simply sought a new trial.

When the Museo Social in Argentina invited him to

give a series of lectures, he saw an opportunity not only to speak but also to escape. It offered good pay and a chance to see his son, Kermit, who had been working in South America. But what truly drew him was a different invitation, one that appealed to his deepest flaw: the belief that salvation was found in the next great challenge.

While Roosevelt was in the region, Brazilian explorer Cândido Rondon asked him to join and assist in planning an expedition to map an uncharted tributary of the Amazon: *Rio da Dúvida* (the River of Doubt). A river over 500 miles long, winding through one of the most hostile environments on earth.

Roosevelt could have declined the invitation. He could have paused long enough to recover from the emotional toll of the campaign and deliberately decide what his next chapter should look like. He could have recognized that a man who had reshaped an entire country did not need another test to validate his worth. But still reeling from the election loss, he was more concerned with outside opinions than with his inner scorecard.

When warned of the inevitable perils of the Amazonian expedition, Roosevelt simply replied, "If it is necessary for me to leave my bones in South America, I am quite ready to do so."

Roosevelt and Rondon assembled a small team made up of Kermit, several American naturalists, and some Brazilian guides. What started as a grand adventure and Roosevelt's next personal challenge quickly became a brutal struggle for survival. Danger lurked around every river bend. Violent rapids, venomous wildlife, disease, hostile indigenous groups, and terrain so dense it had swallowed entire expeditions, all made it quickly apparent why no one had previously mapped the river. But Roosevelt was chasing something: a new test and the emotional high of a challenge big enough to drown out the sting of political failure.

After months in the rainforest, the harsh conditions and treacherous river rapids had left the crew with only two of their seven canoes, dwindling rations, one member of their crew murdered, and another drowned.

Roosevelt contracted malaria and suffered a severe leg infection, leaving him weakened and feverish. Having lost a quarter of his body weight and "hundreds of miles from help, Roosevelt hovered agonizingly on the brink of death. Suffering from disease and starvation, shuddering uncontrollably from fever, the man who had been the youngest and most energetic president in the nation's history drifted in and out of delirium. Too weak to sit up, or even to lift his head."

Coming to terms with the fact that he was going to die in the rainforest, Roosevelt told Kermit and the team to continue without him. Though he had spent much of his life in his father's enormous shadow, in this critical moment, Kermit refused to obey. Faced with his son's resolve not to leave him behind, Roosevelt had no choice but to yield and let the crew carry him.

After months in the jungle, the survivors finally emerged. As Candace Millard describes the team in her book, *The River of Doubt*, "After weeks of surviving on a few bites of fish and a single biscuit each night, they were gaunt and hollow-cheeked. The clothes on their back, the only clothing they had left, were in tatters, and wherever the skin appeared, it was bruised, cut, sunburned, and peppered with insect bites. They were filthy and wild-eyed from disease and fear. And their American commander was barely clinging to life."

They had mapped the river (today called the Roosevelt River), but at extraordinary personal cost. Several men were dead. Many would never fully recover, including Roosevelt himself, who often experienced shortness of breath and chronic pain in his legs. Ultimately, the expedition contributed to his declining health in his final years.

For his entire life, Roosevelt believed the answer to internal turmoil was more intensity: another mountain, another battle, another quest. But the River of Doubt revealed that even the strongest leaders break when they never stop pushing. Even the most resilient body collapses without deliberate rest and renewal. Endurance without reflection becomes recklessness.

Roosevelt could have recovered emotionally after the election loss. By any reasonable measure, he had already lived a life of extraordinary achievement. He could have honored what he had already accomplished rather than chase something new to fill the void. Instead, he sprinted into an expedition that nearly killed him, and that ultimately shortened his life.

Leaders burn out because they ignore their limits, not because they lack courage. They forget that the very strength that makes them effective becomes that which pushes them over the edge.

Great leaders don't simply push hard. They push sustainably and pace themselves. They deliberately recover so they can serve longer, lead better, and remain available for the missions that truly matter.

Rest isn't a reward, it's a requirement. And the courage to continue often begins with the wisdom to pause.

▼

Don't Burn the Steak

In the summer of 1954, legendary coach Paul "Bear" Bryant took his Texas A&M Aggies to Junction, Texas, for a grueling ten-day training camp. The story of the "Junction Boys" has become football mythology – a glorification of toughness and grit. Many coaches still cite Bryant as they take great pride in making "practice tougher than the game."

What often gets lost in the romanticized view of the Junction Boys is what actually happened. During those ten days in the Texas heat, nearly two-thirds of the team either quit or got injured. That season, the Aggies went 1-9 and finished last in the Southwest Conference. While it's true that Bryant eventually turned the program around, very few of the Junction Boys were still on the roster in 1956 when they finished 9-0-1.

At a Junction Boys reunion in 1979, Bryant addressed his former players with unfiltered honesty:

"I never had a team I was more proud of," he said. "I came here today to apologize to y'all. I shouldn't have done what I did to you twenty-five years ago. If somebody had done that to me, I would've just walked off, quit. I really would have."

It's important that we don't take the wrong lessons

from history. It's dangerous to look at the undefeated 1956 Texas A&M team and attribute that success to those ten days of suffering in 1954. The reality is simpler, though less romantic. Bryant recruited better players and refined his preparation methods. Yet countless coaches copied the punishment without understanding the process. Far more failed than succeeded.

Bill Walsh, on the other hand, was extremely concerned with the possibility of "over-training" his athletes. Most coaches in the late 1970s and early 80s used training camp as the time to establish "conditioning and toughness – scrimmages with full contact twice a day, exercise to the point of exhaustion, often using military boot camp as their model."

Contrary to the trends of the time, Bill believed that approach led to "excessive physical and emotional fatigue" that would ultimately result in "decreased concentration, resilience and performance…not to mention higher rates of injury."

Bill shared his concerns with his coaching staff. He didn't want his team entering the season already depleted. Staying fresh physically, mentally, and emotionally was crucial for sustained excellence.

Track coach Tony Holler says, "Don't burn the steak!"

What he means is: don't let today ruin tomorrow. You can always apply more heat later. When you overcook a prime cut, the damage can't be undone. It's a simple statement that serves as a vital reminder to coaches throughout the season.

In addition to wearing down muscles, overtraining fries an athlete's central nervous system. Chronic fatigue increases injury risk, dulls focus, and ultimately can erode confidence. Pulling back requires extreme discipline and awareness from the coach, especially given the temptation to always push athletes for one more rep.

To achieve high performance through deliberate practice, you need to turn up the heat. Practices should be highly competitive, keeping athletes at the edge of their comfort and capability. Turn up the heat, but don't burn the steak. Stress must be paired with recovery. It's a delicate balance, requiring coaches to practice self-control and constant communication with their athletes.

In their book *Peak Performance*, Brad Stulberg and Steve Magness laid out a simple formula:

STRESS + REST = GROWTH

Periods of intense effort should be balanced by periods of rest and recovery. Olympic sprint coaches call this the High/Low approach. If Monday is maximal effort, Tuesday must be lighter.

Bill believed the same. He said, "We never scheduled more than two hard workouts in a row, because I wanted to make sure players did not become so weary that they were unduly vulnerable to muscle pulls, or that their only concern in practice was to survive." The purpose of practice was to improve technique and prepare for the next opponent. If the players were simply surviving practice, they weren't getting better.

Many opposing coaches scoffed at Bill's methods. The NFL in the 1980s was defined by a physical run game and a punishing defense. The only way to prepare was through full-padded, two-a-day practices that tested the courage of every athlete. How could a pass-heavy team with lighter practices win in an era defined by physical brutality?

The 49ers answered on Sundays. Though they went against conventional wisdom, their success was undeniable, and even the most hardened coaches grew to respect Bill for his unique approach.

While Bill was meticulous about managing his players' workload, he was unaware of the load he placed on himself. The exacting standards of excellence eventually led to burnout. He described being up at 3 a.m. many nights, talking into a tape recorder and writing notes on scraps of paper. He was never able to turn off; always looking for an edge. His stress manifested physically, with knots in his stomach and rashes on his skin. He lost his appetite and his sense of humor. He would lie awake worrying about what might go wrong. Worst of all, the constant strain pulled him away from the people he loved most.

Bill loved his work, but the stress eventually got to him. After winning Super Bowl XXIII in 1989, at the height of a dynasty, he walked away from the NFL sidelines and never came back.

It would go down as his greatest professional regret.

"I should have coached a couple more years," Bill reflected, "but it was hard for me to see at the time. If I'd had someone to talk to it wouldn't have taken much to have me stay and just take a furlough for thirty days to clear my head. I think I had more coaching left." While he made sure his players got enough rest, no one made sure he did. As the leader, it can be lonely at the top. For high achievers, the biggest threat to long-term success isn't failure, it's burnout.

In an interview with *The Athletic Football Show*, Los Angeles Rams coach Sean McVay said, "I used to almost think it was cool to get away with not sleeping. That's the dumbest sh*t I've ever heard…When your job is to deal with people, you got to establish healthy habits that are in alignment with sustaining [yourself] when there's a lot of external stressors that the season entails."

Leaders can become so consumed with their team's performance that they neglect many of the behaviors they preach. "Do as I say, not as I do" can only go so far. Over time, the only habits that stick with your team are the ones you embody.

Bill achieved what most coaches can only dream of: he built a dynasty, won multiple Super Bowls, and redefined football strategy. Yet his hardest battle was internal.

He burned out, and it was his greatest regret. After years of building, coaching, innovating, and pushing his team (and himself) to the highest levels, he found that the relentless pace and personal sacrifice had exacted a toll. The very force that fueled his brilliance eventually became a burden. Bill neglected a vital principle: *"Know thyself."*

Knowing thyself isn't just self-awareness; it's understanding your limits, rhythms, and need for deliberate rest. Bill excelled at strategy, fundamentals, and discipline, but he had underestimated the importance of strategically recharging. His routines rarely included extended time off or structured downtime, and over the years, the lack of replenishment diminished his ability to maintain his own peak performance.

Even the most capable leaders require cycles of rest and renewal. Bill's story demonstrates that the cost of ignoring this principle is steep. Burnout impacts more than just you. It affects your team, your decision-making, and the legacy you leave behind.

Sustainable excellence rests on three pillars:

1. **Structured Routines**
   Daily habits that maintain focus
   and reinforce relevant skills.

2. **Purposeful Work**
   Aligning every action with your deepest goals,
   ensuring energy is spent where it matters.

3. **Deliberate Rest and Reflection**
   Sabbaticals, personal reflection, and recovery cycles
   that allow your mind and body to recharge.

Ignore any one of them long enough, and performance erodes.

The measure of greatness is not just how much you can accomplish, but how long you can sustain it. Don't quit your hit show. Don't let the demands of the work you love destroy you. The permanent base camp for excellence is built on effort, discipline, and talent. But also with self-awareness and the courage to pause, rest, recommit, and return stronger. In the midst of your journey to the summit, don't neglect to strategically stop and recover before continuing the climb.

▼

Make Each Day Your Masterpiece

Long before John Wooden became the most successful coach in college basketball history, he was simply the son of an Indiana farmer, shaped by a seven-point creed his father handed him on a card when he was a boy. It read:

1. **Be true to yourself**

2. **Make each day your masterpiece**

3. **Help others**

4. **Drink deeply from good books, especially the Bible**

5. **Make friendship a fine art**

6. **Build a shelter against a rainy day**

7. **Pray for guidance and give thanks for your blessings every day**

Wooden kept that card in his wallet for the rest of his life. Those simple principles later became the foundation for his "Pyramid of Success." But more importantly, they shaped the way he lived and led through a coaching career that spanned over four decades.

A three-time All-American at Purdue University in the early 1930s, Wooden later played professional basketball, coached high school teams in Kentucky and Indiana, and served in the Navy during World War II. Following the war, he spent two years as the coach at Indiana State University before getting the opportunity to coach at The University of California, Los Angeles (UCLA) in 1948.

At the time, UCLA was a .500 program, with just two conference championships in the preceding eighteen years. Leading a team with little national relevance, most coaches would have obsessed over winning immediately. Instead, Wooden focused on building a system that would last. In fact, he never even framed winning as the goal.

"You can lose when you outscore somebody in a game, and you can win when you're outscored." The scoreboard is a lagging indicator – the byproduct of your standards, not the objective itself. Success is being the absolute best that *you* can be. Simon Sinek would later describe the same idea as playing the *infinite game:* measuring progress against your own standard rather than chasing short-term wins. When you play with an inner scorecard, improvement never ends, and neither does the pursuit of excellence.

> **"It's better to travel hopefully than to arrive."**
>
> **- ROBERT LOUIS STEVENSON**

In his first season at UCLA, Wooden led the team to a 22-7 record and a division title. His second year, they won the conference. But his first NCAA championship wouldn't come until 1964, a full sixteen years into his tenure.

Wooden built a culture around mastery of the mundane. One of his most famous routines was teaching his new players how to put on their socks and shoes at the first practice each year. Before even touching a basketball, they needed to understand the importance of the little details.

That little things make big things happen. He'd sit them down in the locker room, remove his own shoes, and demonstrate. No wrinkles in the socks, pull the heel tight, lace the shoes evenly, snug all around the foot. "Imagine each knot is a step towards excellence," he would say. One little wrinkle could result in a blister. A single blister could affect the quality of play on the court. And the quality of play needed to be to the best of their ability at every moment.

Wooden also practiced what Dan Sullivan and Benjamin Hardy have since coined, "Who Not How." It's the idea that big goals are achieved by empowering the right people, not by doing everything yourself.

Wooden trusted and developed his assistants. He thoughtfully delegated the workload and, in the process, developed future head coaches. Larry Brown, Denny Crum, Gene Bartow, and a number of others all went on to lead successful coaching careers after working under Wooden. He believed a well-run system could outlast any single personality, including his own. Empowering his people was one of the principal reasons he could coach at such a high level for decades without burning out.

> *"Renew thyself completely each day; do it again, and again, and forever again."*
> **- HENRY DAVID THOREAU**

From 1964 to 1975, Wooden's Bruins won ten national championships in twelve years, including seven straight, and an 88-game winning streak that still stands as the longest in

NCAA Division I men's basketball history. His teams won nearly 81% of all games across his 27-year tenure at UCLA.

While he coached legends like Lew Alcindor (Kareem Abdul-Jabbar), Bill Walton, Gail Goodrich, and Walt Hazzard, he always insisted he never coached to win. Success, to Wooden, was doing your absolute best, based on an inner scorecard, not an outer one. He acknowledged that success changes expectations. Every championship raised UCLA's baseline. What once felt like a dream season quickly became 'the minimum.' Wooden understood that without an inner scorecard, rising expectations would erode joy and distort purpose. The goalpost always moves, and his Pyramid of Success was designed to decouple identity from external expectations.

Achievement means very little if it costs you everything else.

At age 65, after winning the 1975 NCAA Championship, Wooden announced his retirement. He wasn't burnt out. He simply knew it was time, and he walked away on his own terms. He spent the next 35 years of his life giving lectures, mentoring coaches, writing books, and reflecting on a life well lived.

In line with his father's creed, Wooden truly made every day his masterpiece. And he did it without sacrificing his life in the process.

Section Two

The Process

CARVE OUT

Pottery Class

One year in a pottery class, a teacher announced on the first day that he was dividing the class into two groups. Those on the left side of the studio would be evaluated on the *quantity* of work they produced. Those on the right, solely on *quality.*

At the end of the semester, the teacher would grade the results. The "quantity" group was evaluated entirely on output: how many pots they produced. The "quality" group, meanwhile, needed to produce only a single perfect pot to earn an "A."

When the semester ended, and the pots were laid out for grading, the results surprised everyone. The highest-quality pots all came from the quantity group.

While the quantity group had been churning out pot after pot, learning from mistakes, adjusting techniques, and improving with each attempt, the quality group spent the semester planning. Theorizing about perfection instead of practicing the process. In the end, most produced mediocre work. Others had little to show beyond elegant ideas and a pile of unshaped clay.

Mastery is built through repetition, not intention. Quality emerges from the discipline to keep iterating, not the patience to wait for perfection.

CHAPTER 5

The Way It's ~~Always~~ Never Been Done

"It has never occurred to me to question whether I should do something simply because I haven't done it before."

- SAM ZELLE

"You are remembered for the rules you break."

- DOUGLAS MACARTHUR

"To be nobody but yourself in a world which is doing its best, night and day, to make you everybody else, means to fight the hardest battle which any human being can fight."

- E.E. CUMMINGS

 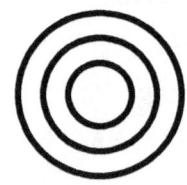 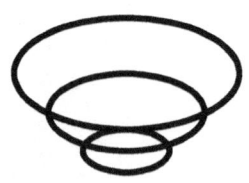

THINK DIFFERENTLY

S ometimes a revolution begins not with a breakthrough, but with a late fee.

In 1997, Reed Hastings returned a copy of *Apollo 13* to Blockbuster and was hit with a $40 late charge. Most people would have grumbled, paid the fee, and moved on. But Hastings questioned the entire system.

"Why does renting a movie have to work this way?"

At the time, the video rental industry was dominated by brick-and-mortar locations. Paying late fees and driving to the store were normal. Everyone assumed the model was untouchable. Netflix began when two founders questioned the assumptions everyone else lived by. And it all started with little experiments.

When Hastings and his co-founder, Marc Randolph, began testing their novel concept, DVDs were new, hard to find, and owned mostly by early adopters. VHS tapes were too bulky to ship cheaply, and the internet was still in its infancy. Still, Hastings and Randolph wondered: *What if movie rentals could happen through the mail?* Everyone in the industry told them their idea would never work.

> *"Everyone who has taken a shower has had an idea. But it's the people who get out of the shower, towel off, and do something about it that make the difference."*
>
> **- NOLAN BUSHNELL**

So they ran an experiment. They bought a used Patsy Cline Greatest Hits CD from a local music shop to mimic a DVD, slipped it inside a birthday card, sealed the accompanying pink envelope, and mailed it to Hastings' home address. When the disk arrived unscathed, they took it as a green light.

What they didn't know was that they had mostly gotten lucky. Months later, Randolph toured their local post office to understand how DVDs would actually be handled. He learned that the Patsy Cline disk had stayed entirely within the local postal loop, which was hand-sorted and relatively gentle. If they had addressed that first disk to anywhere else, automated sorting machines likely would have broken it.

Netflix nearly died before it started, and they didn't even realize it. But their idea was already in motion.

Netflix officially launched on April 14, 1998. Randolph placed the first order himself, requesting a copy of *Casino* to be delivered to his home address outside Scotts Valley, California. Within minutes, the "new order" bell they had coded into the system started ringing nonstop as purchases rolled in. Randolph remembers it sounding like a machine gun. Then their website crashed. The team scrambled to buy eight more computers, relaunched, and the site crashed again after just 45 minutes. They ran out of paper, ink, boxes, and tape.

Managing expectations, they anticipated no more than 20 orders on day one. They ended up with 137, and that was just in the limited windows when the site was actually up. Every mistake became a lesson, and every frustration led to a new experiment. Instead of perfection, they chased progress.

Soon after their launch, shipping became one of their

biggest obstacles. Discs were easily damaged and they constantly fought to trim ounces off the weight of their packages to cut costs. Those ounces added up to pounds, and those pounds resulted in dollars their startup needed to survive.

Late one night in the office, after lamenting over their wildly-over-budget packaging costs, Randolph walked out to his car, grabbed his family's "restaurant bag" filled with "all the distractions needed to get through a meal in public with three children under the age of seven," and got to work. Hacking together prototypes of a new mailer design, Randolph spent hours iterating with the children's craft materials, using cardboard, safety scissors, tape, and crayons until he arrived at the first prototype of what would eventually become Netflix's iconic red envelope. This multimillion-dollar logistics innovation began with a bag of elementary school art supplies. Instead of waiting for the perfect tools, they started with whatever was in front of them.

Netflix survived its first year because Randolph and his team refused to act like a traditional company. They deliberately did the opposite of "the way things have always been done."

When the Bill Clinton grand-jury testimony was released on DVD, Netflix rushed to ship copies for just two cents as a publicity stunt. In the chaos, a handful of adult-content DVDs accidentally got mixed into the batch. Customers opened their mail expecting presidential testimony and got something very different. It was embarrassing. But typical for Netflix, mistakes weren't failures, they were an opportunity to improve. And, funny enough, not a single customer who received the wrong DVD ever bothered to return it.

The real breakthrough came when Netflix confronted a problem that had been bleeding cash for years. By the early 2000s, they had tens of thousands of DVDs sitting idle on warehouse shelves. The economics of the traditional rental model were collapsing. More than just a revenue problem, they had an identity problem.

So they asked a question no one in the industry ever had: If customers clearly want to keep discs longer, why punish them with late fees? Why not design the entire system around that behavior?

Netflix flipped its weakness on its head. Instead of charging fees, they introduced a monthly subscription where customers could hold movies as long as they wanted. Just return one to get the next. It was one of the first large-scale subscription models in home entertainment. A liability became the engine of their explosive growth.

To make it all work, Netflix had to rethink everything: the shipping box, the warehouse layout, the subscription model, and even the mailing system. They challenged every assumption the incumbents lived by. They didn't just "think outside the box," they rebuilt the box entirely. And in doing so, they rebuilt an industry.

In 2007, Netflix made its boldest move yet by launching streaming video. This pivot of abandoning a profitable DVD-by-mail model for a new and unproven technology seemed insane to many at the time, but it cemented the company as a disruptor. Blockbuster, meanwhile, remained tied to its physical stores and traditional revenue streams, eventually declaring bankruptcy in 2010.

What started as a personal annoyance (a $40 late fee) became the seed for one of the most unconventional and transformative business ideas in modern history.

As Randolph put it, "We turned an envelope and a Patsy Cline CD into a publicly traded company."

Netflix didn't succeed because of flawless execution. They succeeded because they experimented relentlessly and refused to do things the way they'd always been done. They questioned every assumption and believed that little improvements compound into breakthroughs.

Ounces equal pounds, pounds become momentum, and momentum turns into a movement.

▼

Reserve the Right to Change Your Mind

A flight from New York City to London's Heathrow Airport takes about seven hours today. But in 1976, you could make the trip in around just three hours aboard the Concorde. It was an engineering marvel, capable of flying Mach 2.04 (more than twice the speed of sound).

While it was a technological breakthrough, it was also a financial disaster. By the time it became available for commercial flight, the British and French governments had invested more than $2 billion into the project. The costs were so high that the aircraft was never profitable. Supersonic transatlantic flights were discontinued in 2003.

The Concorde is a classic example of the sunk cost fallacy: our tendency to continue an endeavor simply because we've already invested time, money, or effort, even when new evidence suggests we shouldn't.

This trap isn't limited to financial decisions. It also shows up in opinions, predictions, and organizational habits. We look for evidence to support our ideas, holding tightly to them even when the empirical evidence says differently.

Bill Walsh was determined to create an environment with the San Francisco 49ers that actively resisted this pitfall. He understood that fear was one of the greatest impediments to clear thinking. If a scout or assistant coach was afraid of being wrong, they would stop communicating, thus withholding valuable information from the team.

"We created an atmosphere in meetings in which a scout or coach was able to express himself completely," Bill explained. "If he overstated or understated in any category, he could change his opinion later without being criticized. We were interested only in results. They could change their mind without being ridiculed. Everyone was expected to participate."

In other words, everyone had permission to say, "I reserve the right to change my mind."

That single principle created enormous freedom.

From the moment Bill arrived in San Francisco, he challenged conventional wisdom. At the time, many NFL coaches were distant authority figures. Bill insisted players call him by his first name. While most teams relied on grueling, marathon practices to prepare for opponents, Bill prioritized shorter bursts of intensity to keep his team fresh. And while some coaches stood atop a tower shouting commands through a megaphone, Bill was on the field, down in the weeds alongside his players. He obsessively studied quarterbacks from the waist down, believing he could predict the outcome of a play by their footwork alone.

These weren't gimmicks. They were expressions of a leader willing to rethink everything.

That mindset showed up clearly in the 1979 NFL Draft.

Bill was focused on finding a quarterback to operate his offensive system. While he ended up selecting Notre Dame's Joe Montana in the 3rd round, initially, he was intrigued by Clemson quarterback Steve Fuller. Standing 6'4" with a strong arm, Fuller looked the part and possessed the traits most franchises were looking for in a future starting quarterback.

Bill flew to Clemson, South Carolina to see Fuller throw. When he called the apartment, Fuller's roommate, Dwight Clark, picked up the phone. Clark caught only twelve passes during his senior year. No one considered him an NFL prospect, but Bill invited him to catch a few passes from Fuller during the workout.

It didn't take long for Bill to decide that Fuller wasn't his guy. According to author David Harris, "[Bill] thought most scouts had little idea of what made a quarterback successful and placed far too much value on arm strength and physical stature." While Bill had passed on Fuller, he walked away from the workout extremely impressed by his unheralded roommate.

Though Clark lacked production in college, at 6'4", 215 pounds, Bill could envision a role for him in the San Francisco offense. "I was looking for a big receiver who could go against linebackers and catch the short and medium-range passes underneath coverage and I thought he would be an excellent candidate." Bill drafted Clark in the 10th round, who went on to become an All-Pro receiver and two-time Super Bowl champion.

In his book, *The Genius*, Harris recalled, "Predicting success in football, as Walsh did, was a three-dimensional process requiring not only an assessment of athletic talent but also the ability to project a player into the situation in which he would be used." Bill evaluated players not against generic standards, but against how he intended to use them.

Writer Elbert Hubbard said, "To escape criticism, do nothing, say nothing, be nothing." Many coaches in the early 1980s were following the consensus. They ran the same schemes and shared similar evaluations of talent in the upcoming draft. Bill was not willing to accept conventional thinking. He knew that conviction was necessary in order to turn around the 49ers. "I instructed everyone scouting that I wanted to know what the redeeming quality is that this person has that will help us win," Bill explained. "Don't just tell me what he can't do. Tell me what he *can* do."

By aligning scouts and coaches around a shared vision, the 49ers built a roster no one else would have assembled. Bill wasn't playing someone else's game. He was designing his own.

Bill drafted running backs Roger Craig and Tom Rathman, who both had a "reputation of being unable to catch the ball when they were in college, but that was because Nebraska had a run-oriented offense and never threw to the backs." It wasn't that they couldn't catch the ball; they simply hadn't been given the opportunity. Bill saw what others missed, and they became two of the most dynamic receiving running backs the league had seen.

Don't tell me what they can't do. Tell me what they can do.

Bill also drafted undersized, mobile offensive linemen because they fit his offense. "[Bill] wasn't picking players for someone else to coach but players he would put to use himself." Don't play everyone else's game. Don't think like everyone else. Have a clear vision and put it into action.

"I reserve the right to change my mind" didn't mean being indecisive. It meant holding strong convictions while remaining open to better information.

Great leaders aren't contrarian for the sake of being different. They're willing to question inherited assumptions, absorb new evidence, and act decisively when others hesitate. They don't make decisions by polling the court of public opinion. They hold deep convictions, while remaining flexible enough to upgrade their ideas. They are constantly asking, *Is there a better way to do this?*

Bill wasn't trying to be different. He was trying to be better. The leaders who change the game are simply more willing to think for themselves.

▼

Only Governments Can Do That

Since the Great Space Race of the 1950s and '60s, progress in space exploration had slowed dramatically. Rockets became vastly more expensive but not meaningfully better. Launch costs regularly exceeded $10,000 per pound, and aerospace had become a stagnant industry dominated by a handful of government contractors. By the early 2000s, rocketry was more bureaucracy than it was engineering. Until Elon Musk set out to disrupt the industry.

Before becoming widely known as an eccentric billionaire and controversial public figure, Musk was a successful technology entrepreneur with no background in aerospace. Despite his lack of credentials, in 2002, Musk announced that humanity needed a path to Mars. Aerospace veterans scoffed. Even some of his most successful friends begged him not to waste his fortune chasing a "science fiction project." Rockets were the domain of governments and legacy giants like Boeing and Lockheed Martin, not internet entrepreneurs.

> ### *"I want to die on Mars, just not on impact."*
> - ELON MUSK

But Musk didn't see an industry of brilliance, he saw an industry of unquestioned assumptions. So he started asking different questions:

Why do rockets cost so much? Why can't parts be built in-house? Why can't rockets be reused?

He read every rocket-engineering biography he could find. He called retired engineers and borrowed their old manuals. When SpaceX began, he interviewed the first 3,000 employees himself, prioritizing curiosity over credentials.

Traditional aerospace followed a rigid, linear development model: design for years, build slowly, test cautiously, and avoid failure at all costs. After all, failures were incredibly expensive. SpaceX inverted all of that. At their first facility in Hawthorne, California, engineers worked in a warehouse-like environment where prototypes were built in days, not months. Musk would often walk the floor at 2 am, pushing teams to run another test, fix the problem, and test again before dawn. Every experiment was a chance to learn. Every explosion was a data point to keep improving.

One early engineer at SpaceX contrasted it with his friend at Lockheed Martin, whose entire job was sourcing a single bolt for the F-35 fighter jet. His friend was working in the old world: narrow, slow, compartmentalized. SpaceX was fast, took risks, and did everything differently.

While designing their first rocket, Musk and his engineers ran into a problem that would define their entire philosophy: the aerospace supply chain was slow, overpriced, and averse to innovation.

During the design of the Falcon 1 rocket, SpaceX's engineers needed a valve for the mechanism that steered the rocket by adjusting engine direction. Traditional aerospace suppliers quoted them $25,000 per part, with delivery times stretching months. This wasn't unusual in the industry. Aerospace parts were expensive because they were "aerospace parts," built by a handful of approved vendors with long government contracts. Nobody questioned it. Except Musk.

When asked, the suppliers didn't have a real explanation. It was simply the accepted aerospace way, defined by massive markups, slow lead times, and unquestioned legacy processes. Musk pushed back. If SpaceX was going to survive, they couldn't build rockets the way everyone else did. They had to rethink every assumption, every supplier relationship, every part.

So instead of buying the valve, SpaceX decided to manufacture it themselves. Their small team reverse-engineered the design, built custom tooling, selected new materials, and machined the valve in-house. When they were done, they had produced a fully functional valve that met the same performance requirements for less than $1,000. And they delivered it in weeks, not months.

If a single valve could be made better, cheaper, and faster by ignoring convention, what else could they build differently? The answer, it turned out, was everything.

SpaceX began manufacturing fuel pumps, engine components, and structural assemblies, parts that the industry believed could only be sourced from legacy contractors. In many cases, SpaceX's parts weren't just cheaper; they were higher performing, because the engineers designing them could walk across the factory floor and collaborate directly with the machinists building them. Iteration happened in days rather than years.

But proving that these innovations worked required more than a whiteboard and a factory floor, it required launching rockets from one of the most isolated places on earth.

When SpaceX relocated its launches from Texas to the remote U.S. Army base on Kwajalein Atoll (Kwaj), the team spent months shipping 30 tons of equipment across the Pacific. Located in the Republic of the Marshall Islands, roughly halfway between Hawaii and Australia, the island was so remote that supplies took a month to arrive by boat. Engineers slept in shipping containers, sweating through tropical humidity, fighting mosquitoes, and building a launch site from scratch.

Then, after all the obstacles they had already overcome, the launches began to go wrong. Falcon 1 Flights 1, 2, and 3 all failed. Each one was publicly humiliating and financially devastating. At the same time, Musk's other project, Tesla, was burning through cash and nearing bankruptcy.

When most founders would have quit, Musk pushed forward. He had already poured more than $100 million of his own money into SpaceX, leaving room for one final attempt to reach orbit. And survival depended on more than a successful launch. They needed NASA's attention to secure a contract that would determine whether the company lived or died. So Musk decided to make them notice.

SpaceX engineers built a full-scale 68-foot Falcon rocket replica that was hollow inside, but visually identical to the real launch vehicle. Then, they loaded the rocket onto a flatbed truck and drove it straight down Independence Avenue in Washington, D.C. The rocket was finally parked directly across the street from the National Air and Space Museum, very close to the NASA headquarters. If NASA wouldn't return their calls, maybe they would respond to a rocket parked outside their front door.

On September 28, 2008, after their team spent years sleeping in shipping containers, hand-building components, and enduring failure after failure, Falcon 1 Flight 4 lifted off from Kwaj and reached orbit. It became the first privately developed, liquid-fueled rocket in history to do so.

The success came just weeks before SpaceX would have run out of money entirely.

That single launch unlocked a $1.6 billion NASA contract and rewrote the future of commercial spaceflight. From there, SpaceX accelerated at a pace few believed possible.

They built the Falcon 9, proving rockets could be reused and dramatically lowering the cost of access to space.

They developed the Dragon capsule, meant to ferry cargo, and eventually astronauts, to the International Space Station (ISS). Then SpaceX raised the bar again with Starship, the largest rocket ever built.

By 2023, the U.S. share of global commercial launch revenue, once near zero, had risen to 54%, with SpaceX responsible for the majority.

SpaceX succeeded because of a refusal to accept inherited wisdom. They embraced experimentation, encouraged failure, iterated relentlessly, and hired people who would challenge old ideas rather than defend them.

Industries don't change because someone has a good idea. They change when someone is bold enough to question what everyone else accepts as fact. SpaceX didn't win because they were smarter; they won because they did things the way they've never been done.

CHAPTER 6

The Power of Constraints

"The enemy of art is the absence of limitation."

- **ORSON WELLES**

"Perfection is achieved, not when there is nothing more to add, but when there is nothing left to take away."

- **ANTOINE DE SAINT-EXUPÉRY**

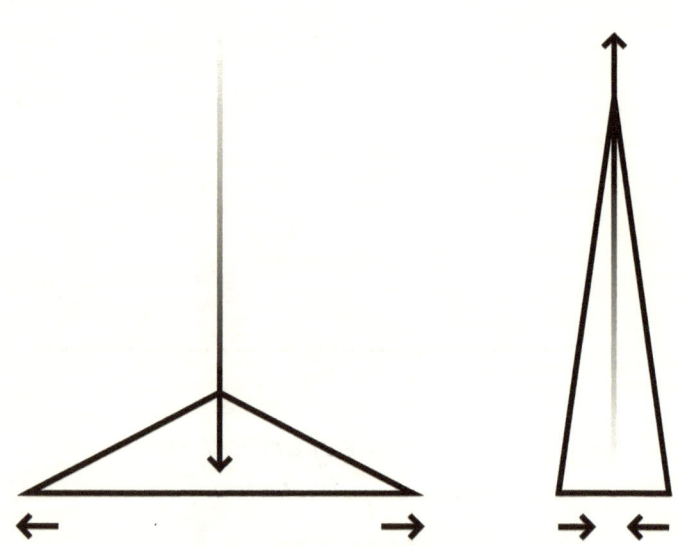

CONSTRAINTS DRIVE CREATIVITY

In the restaurant world, the instinct is always to offer more. More menu items, more options, more ways to appeal to everyone. Especially for a new restaurant fighting to survive. But Todd Graves did the opposite. He built an empire by offering less.

Graves opened Raising Cane's with just four core menu items: chicken fingers, crinkle-cut fries, Texas toast, and coleslaw. No burgers, salads, or seasonal milkshakes.

What looked like a limitation became his greatest advantage. The simple menu created operational clarity. With fewer moving parts, every process could be refined to near perfection. Training employees was simpler and supply chains were more efficient. Simplicity turned into mastery of the few key variables. Creativity flourished because there were constraints, not in spite of them. Customers always knew what they were getting and the employees always knew how to deliver it.

> **"You don't need a lot of choices to make something memorable. You need focus."**
>
> **- TODD GRAVES**

But the idea didn't start as brilliance. It started as the lowest grade on a class assignment.

As a student at Louisiana State University (LSU), Graves and his original business partner wrote a plan for a chicken-finger-only restaurant (originally called Folley's Fingers). After presenting their idea to the class, not only did the professor tell them their idea wouldn't work, but they also received the worst grade in the class. Like many other "voices of reason" at the time, they were advised to serve more variety to appease a broader audience.

Undeterred, Graves pushed forward. He bought a cheap suit and a boxy briefcase with brass combination locks. In the briefcase he placed his "secret recipe" and guarded it like a treasure that everyone was trying to steal. What the briefcase actually contained was his business plan, the very one that won him the worst grade in the class.

He then went to every bank in town, toting the briefcase, and trying to find enough money to get their first location off the ground. Despite his clever marketing, which won them a few conversations and drew some attention, all the bankers recommended that he gain a decade of industry experience before trying to start his own chain.

Seeing no other choice, Graves set out to create his own capital. He spent the summer working the highest-paying, most dangerous jobs he could find. He started as a boilermaker in an oil refinery, then as a commercial fisherman in Alaska.

While grinding through 20-hour days and saving every dollar, he talked openly about his "chicken finger dream" to anyone who would listen. A few of the boilermakers believed in him enough to invest. To this day, they remain the only outside investors Raising Cane's has ever had.

With their support, an SBA loan, and the money from those brutal jobs, Graves opened the first Raising Cane's in 1996 just outside the north gates of LSU. He lived in an apartment behind the restaurant, named the business after his dog, and committed to a single philosophy:

"Do one thing, and do it better than anyone."

That constraint became his competitive superpower.

When Hurricane Katrina devastated the Gulf Coast in 2005, 21 of the 28 Raising Cane's locations were damaged and forced to close. Facing the looming possibility of going out of business entirely, Graves rallied his teams to be the first restaurant to reopen and serve local communities. Their simplicity enabled speed, allowing them to pivot quickly and restore operations, while competitors struggled under complexity.

By 2025, Raising Cane's surpassed 900 locations. At that point, the company averaged roughly $6.5 million in revenue per store, more than any major chain except Chick-fil-A.

Graves never expanded the menu or chased trends. He never wandered from the constraint that enabled him to be great.

As David Oglvy wrote, "What guts it takes, what obstinate determination to stick to one coherent, creative policy year after year, in the face of all the pressure to come up with something new."

When asked how Raising Cane's grew so large from such a small idea, Graves simply replied: *"Nothing ever happens unless someone pursues a vision fanatically."*

Constraints don't limit success. They are a key ingredient.

And often, the question for a business isn't, "How is it different?" It's the much harder question: "How is it *better*?"

Find a simple idea and take it very seriously. Then turn the constraints into your competitive advantage.

▼

The West Coast Offense

In 1968, a 3M research scientist named Spencer Silver was attempting to develop a new adhesive for the aerospace industry. His goal was straightforward, "to develop bigger, stronger, tougher adhesives," said Silver. What he created was the opposite. "This was none of those," Silver later admitted. The adhesive was weak and barely sticky. Chalking it up as a failure, it sat unused until another 3M scientist, Art Fry, had a eureka moment:

"Every Wednesday night while practicing with his church choir, he would use little scraps of paper to mark the hymns they were going to sing in the upcoming service. By Sunday, he'd find that they'd all fallen out of the hymnal. He needed a bookmark that would stick to the paper without damaging the pages."

Fry remembered Silver's "not very sticky" adhesive and thought it would be the perfect solution to his hymnal bookmark problem. Before long, the Post-it Note would become a productivity staple in almost every office. Silver said that, like many ground-breaking innovations, theirs was a product nobody thought they needed until it existed.

The invention of the Post-it Note is one of Bill Walsh's favorite stories because it captured one of his deepest beliefs: "Be obsessive in finding the upside in the downside."

Constraints often look like setbacks, but they can become catalysts for better outcomes. When facing a limitation, lean into it. Turn it into your superpower.

Bill's invention of the "West Coast Offense" was born not from a master plan, but from constraint. In 1969, he was the offensive coordinator for the Cincinnati Bengals. The head coach and owner, Paul Brown, selected Greg Cook with the fifth overall pick in the draft. Cook was the platonic ideal for the quarterback position: 6'4", 220 pounds, and a cannon arm. Immediately installed as the starter, the Bengals began dominating their competition. Under Bill's tutelage, Cook took the league by storm.

Three games into the season, the undefeated Bengals played the Kansas City Chiefs. During the game, Cook scrambled to his left and attempted to duck under the tackle of Chiefs linebacker Greg Lynch. Landing awkwardly, he felt a searing pop in his shoulder. He would later learn that he had torn his rotator cuff and partially detached his bicep muscle. The injury was devastating, and Cook would never fully recover.

The Bengals were left with backup quarterback Virgil Carter. A sixth-round draft pick out of Brigham Young University (BYU), he was well known for leading the team to a conference championship in 1965 using a precision passing attack, though they had historically been a run-heavy, single-wing offense.

Carter was smart and an accurate passer, but he had one of the weakest arms in the league. The Bengals already lacked a power running game; now they also lacked a vertical passing threat. Conventional wisdom offered few solutions.

So Bill created one. Rather than lament what Carter couldn't do, Bill redesigned the offense around what he could. Instituting a form of ball-control offense through the air, the Bengals focused on short, precision passes designed to maintain possession and create long drives. Timing, accuracy, and rhythm became the foundation. What emerged was a passing game that functioned like a running game. The West Coast Offense was the result of a limitation turned into an advantage. And it would become the foundational system for most NFL play callers in the years to follow.

"While waiting to get what you want," Bill said, "make the most of what you got." Coaches and leaders often learn the most when they are faced with constraints. Carter's physical limitations forced Bill to think differently, to find a path to maximize the talent he possessed. Over time, Bill refined the system with Ken Anderson in Cincinnati, Steve Dils at Stanford, and eventually Joe Montana and Steve Young in San Francisco. What began as a desperate response to injury became the dominant offensive philosophy of the 1980s.

Don't waste your mistakes. Don't ignore your mishaps. Don't spend time lamenting your bad luck. In the face of any limitation, there is still a path to success. The best leaders are problem solvers.

Charles Darwin wrote of Natural Selection as the "survival of the fittest." The organisms with the best genetic traits survived and passed those traits down to the next generation. Over time, the "good" genes thrived, and the "bad" genes died.

Football innovation has experienced a similar evolution of ideas. The good ideas are passed on and tweaked as coaches seek success and survival. What starts as a limitation can become an asset when a creative coach relentlessly iterates on the idea.

In studying the game of football, it's clear that some of the most significant innovations came as a byproduct of dealing with unanticipated constraints. The examples are too numerous to list, but two that stand out are the Split Back Veer and the Zone Read:

Bill Yeoman - The Split Back Veer

In 1964, the University of Houston was preparing to face a strong Penn State team. The Cougars were in the midst of a dismal 2-6-1 season under third-year head coach Bill Yeoman. During practice, Yeoman was trying to run a simple "Dive" play against the eight-man front they would see employed by Penn State. Even the scout team was dismantling the Houston offense.

Frustrated, Yeoman yelled to his offensive tackle, "Since you can't block the guy, just get out of the way!"

Much to his surprise, the unblocked defender repeatedly ran himself out of the play. The next morning, Yeoman studied the practice film and realized he had stumbled onto something powerful. The "Veer" play could be schematic gold.

Penn State would ultimately win the game, but Houston piled up offensive yardage, revealing what was possible with the new concept.

The Houston "Split Back Veer" went on to revolutionize offensive football. Yeoman's teams led the nation in total offense for three consecutive seasons in the 1960s. The system later powered Bob Ladouceur's De La Salle High School teams to 399 total wins and influenced Art Briles' "Veer & Shoot" offense that reshaped college football in the 2010s.

Decades of dominance traced back to a simple constraint: the offensive line couldn't block. Instead of fighting that reality, Yeoman embraced it, turning limitation into a defining feature.

Rich Rodriguez - The Zone Read

In 1991, Rich Rodriguez was the head coach at Division II Glenville State in rural West Virginia. Like most small programs, they didn't have elite linemen or prototypical quarterbacks. Rodriguez had to find ways to manufacture advantages with what he had.

As the story goes, "An inadvertent epiphany came during a practice when quarterback Jed Drenning bobbled a handoff, gathered himself, and made a split-second decision to run after seeing the defensive end pinch inside."

Under normal circumstances, the mistake would have been corrected. The quarterback would be told to follow the running back and salvage a few yards. But when Drenning spontaneously decided to take off outside, Rodriguez saw the potential. The defense had overcommitted to the running back and the quarterback's mistake exposed it.

Rather than fixing the error, Rodriguez built around it. Their initial constraints of nontraditional personnel and imperfect execution were transformed into schematic advantages. If the defender crashed, the quarterback kept the ball. If he stayed wide, the ball was handed off. A limitation in practice became the foundation of the Zone Read.

The innovation turned Glenville State into a Division II powerhouse and propelled Rich Rodriguez to the head coaching job at West Virginia. There, with dynamic quarterback Pat White, explosive running back Steve Slaton, and the sledgehammer of a fullback Owen Schmidt, the Zone Read scaled into one of the most formidable offenses in college football history.

Innovation doesn't come from ideal conditions. It comes from constraints that force adaptation.

In his book *Orthodoxy*, G.K. Chesterton captured it best: "Art is limitation; the essence of every picture is the frame." Constraints define the canvas. The possibilities are not endless. And it's better this way. It requires focus that breeds innovation. Make peace with your limitations and use them to your advantage. Let them spark your creativity.

Once you've defined your canvas, you can begin to create. Be obsessive in finding the upside in the downside. Like Bill in the early years of creating the West Coast Offense, once you accept the limits of what you have, you're free to build something that changes the game.

▼

Just 50 Words

Having published several classic books, such as *The Cat in the Hat* and *Horton Hears a Who!*, Dr. Seuss (Ted Geisel) had earned quite the name for himself by the late 1950s. His books were beloved, but he had yet to create the book that would define his career. That moment came from an unexpected place: a constraint.

His editor at Random House, Bennett Cerf, bet that he couldn't write an entire children's book using fewer than 50 unique words. The idea grew out of a new educational initiative aiming to improve early reading skills. The goal was to create books with simple, repetitive vocabulary that made reading feel approachable rather than intimidating. Most authors saw the limitation as suffocating. Dr. Seuss saw it as a game.

> **"I like nonsense, it wakes up the brain cells. Fantasy is a necessary ingredient in living."**
>
> **- DR. SEUSS**

The constraint forced him to strip away excess and focus on rhythm, repetition, and pure imagination. With so few words to work with, every phrase mattered. Instead of resisting, he leaned in, viewing the challenge as an opportunity to experiment and find joy within the boundaries.

Rumored to have only taken him a few weeks, Dr. Seuss wrote *Green Eggs and Ham*, a book even more restrictive than *The Cat in the Hat*, which used only 236 words. Its simplicity made it unforgettable. Kids and parents both loved reading it, and it was passed down through generations.

Green Eggs and Ham went on to sell more than 200 million copies worldwide, making it Dr. Seuss's best-selling book and one of the most iconic children's books ever written. What began as a restrictive challenge ultimately produced his most enduring work. The limitation unlocked creation.

Constraints often feel like obstacles. Like shackles that narrow options and stifle imagination. *But the art is in what you leave out.*

Dr. Seuss's story is proof that constraints can be catalysts for innovation. The boundaries forced him to think differently and focus on the essence of what made his writing special.

Sometimes the most powerful creativity doesn't come from thinking outside the box, but from discovering what's possible *inside* one.

CHAPTER 7

Be The Expert

"Success is a few simple disciplines, practiced every day; while failure is simply a few errors in judgement, repeated every day."

- JIM ROHN

"A master in the art of living draws no sharp distinction between his work and his play; his labor and his leisure; his mind and his body; his education and his recreation."

- ATTRIBUTED TO LAO TZU

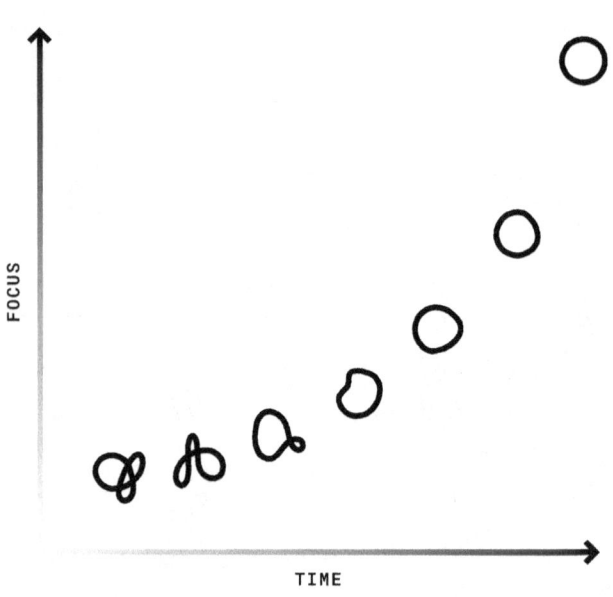

MASTER YOUR CRAFT

In the mountainous Wardak Province in the central region of Afghanistan, a special operations Ranger assault force was doing what they do best – conducting a raid to capture or kill high value enemy targets. It was a hot, dark night in the summer of 2019, and while Ranger missions are inherently risky, no one anticipated the unprecedented actions this one would call for. What followed became one of the clearest demonstrations of what real expertise looks like: mastery under pressure, performed by people who've trained so relentlessly that excellence becomes instinct.

As the assault force cleared the target compound, they were hit with machine-gun fire from several enemy fighting positions. While maneuvering on a suspected barricaded shooter, a large explosion ripped through the breach (the tactical forced entry point), injuring several Rangers. When the dust and debris finally settled, the Ranger Combat Medics got to work.

While chaos ensued around them, the medics triaged the wounded, directing their Advanced Ranger First Responder (ARFR) certified teammates – the 75th Ranger Regiment's equivalent to emergency medical technicians – to continue medical treatment on those with less severe wounds. As one of the medics made his way through the compound alongside another Ranger and an Afghan partner force soldier, they saw another casualty lying on the ground, unnaturally contorted. Without hesitating, they pulled him behind cover from the enemy gunfire to assess his condition.

After placing several tourniquets on the wounded Ranger's arm, leg, and pelvis, the medic cut off his body armor to find a gaping hole in his chest. He then started an intravenous (IV) line, administered medication to prevent heavy bleeding, and began transfusing the first of two units of cold-stored whole blood, which every Ranger medic carries into combat.

They quickly moved the injured Ranger to the casualty collection point (CCP). Even there, they continued receiving enemy machine-gun fire, and a fragmentation grenade detonated just fifteen meters away. Wearing full combat equipment and lying in the dirt, the medics performed several advanced procedures to keep the casualties alive.

The firefight around them was so intense, the medics repeatedly shielded their teammates with their own bodies as large rounds impacted just thirty meters from their position. "With all the available whole blood units already administered to the casualties, [the medics] determined the critically wounded man would die from blood loss if they didn't take action." So they decided to implement the Ranger O-Low Titer (ROLO) protocol.

The ROLO program is a novel medical system, created by the 75th Ranger Regiment, that allows one Soldier to transfer his or her blood to a wounded Soldier in just a few minutes on the battlefield. Rather than relying on the limited amount of cold-stored blood medics can carry, the program tracks the unit's universal donor volunteers (O blood type) to provide large quantities of whole blood as the situation requires. Effectively, a mobile blood bank.

In under ten minutes, blood is drawn from one of the predetermined donors, who can then return to combat while that blood is immediately administered to the casualty. The program has since spread to other service branches (such as the Navy's Valkyrie program) and fundamentally transformed how the military treats catastrophic battlefield injuries.

That night in Afghanistan, the Ranger's injuries were so extensive that medics implemented the ROLO protocol multiple times while awaiting helicopter evacuation. By the time he reached the hospital for continued care, *more Ranger blood flowed through his veins than his own.*

The Ranger Medics ultimately saved several lives that night while repeatedly risking their own. Without their skill and composure under fire, the critically wounded Rangers would not have left the objective alive. Every one of them survived. The medics embodied the Ranger Creed, refusing to "leave a fallen comrade," and truly "shouldering more than their share of the task, whatever it may be, one-hundred-percent and then some."

The 75th Ranger Regiment has had *zero* preventable combat deaths since instituting Ranger First Responder (RFR), its standardized combat medical training course. This is remarkable in a combat environment where uncontrolled hemorrhage (often non-compressible) remains the leading cause of potentially survivable battlefield fatalities.

The life-saving ROLO protocol the Ranger Medics performed on that dark night in 2019 marked the first documented time it had ever been performed in combat.

While the procedure doesn't require cutting edge medical technology, it does require relentless discipline and an uncompromising standard of excellence. A standard that Rangers are known for. Mastery comes from countless hours of practice in combat-simulated environments, preparing medics to perform under the worst possible conditions:

under fire, in full kit, on the ground, and in the dark.

Nothing can fully prepare someone for moments like that. But dedication to excellence and impeccably high standards across the unit allow the 75th Ranger Regiment to do what others can't.

Chartered by General Creighton Abrams to be "elite, light, and the most proficient infantry in the world," the Rangers are highly regarded as one of the most disciplined and capable fighting forces that exists. The medics who fought in Wardak lived that charter to its fullest. They didn't improvise greatness. They practiced it thousands of times before they ever saw combat.

They truly are the experts. Masters of their craft.

▼

Be (More) Specific

Swedish psychologist Anders Ericsson published a famous study that was later popularized by Malcolm Gladwell in his book, *Outliers*. Gladwell's interpretation suggested that it takes roughly 10,000 hours of practice to master a complex skill.

Ericsson later clarified his findings in *Peak: Secrets from the New Science of Expertise*. Studying elite ballet dancers from the Bolshoi Ballet in Russia and violinists from the Berlin Philharmonic, one thing became clear: "We found no shortcuts and no 'prodigies' who reached expert level with relatively little practice." Time alone was not enough.

What mattered was the deliberate, painstaking practice

of each individual technique, guided by exceptional teachers. Ericsson found that those who progressed fastest weren't just practicing more, they were practicing *better*. To make dramatic improvements through practice, Ericsson wrote, "you need a teacher or coach who assigns practice techniques designed to help you improve on very specific skills."

> *"Never mistake activity for achievement."*
>
> **– JOHN WOODEN**

That responsibility places a unique demand on leaders.

High-level coaches must be able to zoom out and see the big picture. They can't "miss the forest for the trees." But they must also be willing to zoom all the way in, down to the intricate details, and get "lost in the weeds" when necessary. There is a time for strategic vision, and a time for obsessive focus. Mastery requires both perspectives.

Decades before Ericsson's research was published, Bill Walsh was already practicing these same principles. He famously said, "With hard work on mechanics and techniques, you can measurably develop a man's consistency." He meant that literally.

As an example:

"After careful analysis, [the Offensive Line Coaches] identified thirty specific and separate physical skills – actions – that every Offensive Lineman needed to master in order to do his job at the highest level, everything from tackling to evasion, footwork to arm movement. Our coaches then created multiple drills for each one of those individual skills, which were practiced relentlessly until their execution at the highest level was automatic – routine 'perfection.'"

Precision was the key. Not complexity.

One of Bill's greatest strengths was his ability to break audacious goals into their component parts. As an offensive play caller, he needed to see the whole field and strategically choreograph all eleven players. But as a teacher, he had to diagnose individual breakdowns and provide precise, technical feedback to every position.

Zoom out to teach the group. Zoom in to develop the individual.

At every level, Bill was teaching. And he had the expertise to support it.

Just over thirty miles away, separated by the San Francisco Bay Bridge, that same philosophy was taking shape in another program.

Bob Ladouceur, the legendary football coach at De La Salle High School, began his tenure in 1979, the same year Bill took over the 49ers. From 1992 to 2004, Ladouceur led the De La Salle Spartans to twelve consecutive undefeated seasons, setting a national record for high school football of 151 consecutive wins.

When asked the secret to such sustained excellence, Ladouceur didn't mention the weight room, the off-season program, or highly effective team-building activities. He said the key to success was *specific football knowledge*.

If his players ever had a question, he either had the

answer or he went and found it immediately. His job as a coach was to be a problem-solver for his athletes and communicate clearly, always putting them in the best position to make plays on Friday nights.

> *"A good leader is always learning. The great leaders start learning young and continue until their last breath."*
>
> - BILL WALSH

Bill operated the same way. He was the ultimate problem solver. Countless times throughout his career, when faced with a daunting challenge, he found a creative solution.

In January of 1982, the 49ers faced the New York Giants and their sensational rookie linebacker, Lawrence Taylor, in the playoffs. To most offensive linemen in the NFL, Taylor was unblockable. With his speed and violence, he routinely harassed and sacked opposing quarterbacks. Bill had built his team around a smaller, more mobile offensive line to fit his system. As a result, his left tackle didn't stand a chance trying to block Taylor.

So Bill went to work. He spent hours with assistant coach Bobb McKittrick coming up with a game plan. They finally decided on "pulling left guard John Ayers in passing situations" to handle Taylor. At 6'5", 270 pounds, Ayers was the 49ers' best pass protector, and Bill found a creative way to create the best match up on Taylor. Then he scripted seventeen passes in the first twenty-two plays to neutralize the Giants' rush.

The plan worked to perfection. The 49ers won, and

would go on to win the Super Bowl that year.

Bill later said, "The very basis of coaching is the knowledge you possess and how well it is imparted."

Coaching is teaching. Coaching is problem-solving. Coaching is knowing your field so thoroughly that you can put your people in the best position to succeed.

The only way to help others find success is by becoming a master of your craft.

There is no shortcut to mastery. You can't fake expertise. If you have the answer, give it with confidence. If you don't, don't pretend you do. Be relentless in your pursuit of knowledge for the sake of those you lead.

If it's possible to be more specific, you should be more specific.

Sun Tzu wrote, "With more sophistication comes more control." Bill believed that "the more you work at refining your teaching – increasing its sophistication – the greater your control of the teaching (and learning) process."

That distinction matters. The goal is not to make teaching more complicated. It is to make it more usable. The sophistication of your teaching methods is not used to control the player, it's used to control the process. The more specific you are when you teach, the more usable information you are giving your athletes.

Too many leaders try to control people instead of controlling the learning process. Better teachers make better students, and better students make better teachers. It becomes a flywheel of curiosity, problem-solving, and sophistication.

High-level leaders are always teaching. The best leaders continually refine their teaching methods.

Specificity requires expertise. And the only way to be more specific is to know more.

▼

Sweat the (Right) Small Stuff

In *Atomic Habits*, James Clear recounts the transformation of British Cycling from mediocrity to world-class performance. It began with hiring performance director Dave Brailsford, who quickly installed his philosophy: "the aggregation of marginal gains."

Find the smallest advantages in unlikely places.

Here are a few of their small adjustments that contributed to success:

- Redesigned the bike seats to make them more comfortable.

- Rubbed alcohol on the tires for better grip.

- Tested various fabrics in a wind tunnel and had their outdoor riders switch to lighter and more aerodynamic indoor racing suits.

- Hired a surgeon to teach each rider the best way to wash their hands to reduce the chances of illness.

- Determined the type of pillow and mattress that led to the best night's sleep.

They even "painted the inside of the team truck white, which helped them spot little bits of dust that would normally slip by unnoticed but could degrade the performance of the finely tuned bikes." Notice the details. Make problems visible. Then fix them quickly.

These are examples of sweating the right kind of small stuff that translates to improved performance.

James Clear notes, "As these and hundreds of other small improvements accumulated, the results came faster than anyone could have imagined."

British Cycling went on to dominate multiple Olympic Games and win dozens of World Championships in the decade following Dave Brailsford's hiring. His methods didn't win public praise, but they transformed the culture. Little things led to big wins.

When Curt Cignetti rebuilt Indiana football from the bottom of the Big Ten to number one in the nation, he famously said he would "stalk complacency" and root it out. The principle is the same. If you want to remove bad habits from your team, you need to make them easy to spot. What's visible gets corrected, and what gets corrected becomes the standard.

Bill was keenly aware of the attention to detail necessary to create sustained success. He was meticulous about sweating the *right* small stuff. Famous for diagramming his plays with architectural precision, every pass pattern had an exact depth that was tied to the quarterback's footwork. This level of detail is standard practice now, but it was revolutionary in 1979.

In football, inches are often the difference between victory and defeat. And Bill accounted for every inch. But he also warned against misdirected obsession. If something doesn't impact performance, you might be sweating (the wrong) small stuff.

In a highly competitive profession, some leaders engage in "productive procrastination." They redesign the flow of the lunchroom or obsess over the pre-game alignment for the National Anthem. While these activities may feel productive, not every detail impacts performance. Don't waste time polishing what doesn't matter.

Elite performers channel their neuroticism toward meaningful gains, not distractions disguised as productivity. Mastery isn't about doing more. It's about knowing exactly what matters and relentlessly refining it.

Bill's lifelong devotion to expertise, coupled with his insistence on that same standard throughout the organization, culminated in the 49ers' near-perfect season in 1984. They finished 15-1, becoming the first team to win fifteen games in the sixteen-game schedule. Their lone loss came by just three points. They went on to dominate the Miami Dolphins in the Super Bowl, capping a season widely regarded as one of the greatest in NFL history.

Elite coaches take great pride in their craft. They become experts, not to elevate themselves, but to serve their people. Trust is built when people know you will solve the right problems, with precision, when it counts.

▼

Warren Buffett and Salad Oil

Being an expert doesn't mean having all the answers. It means knowing how to find them, knowing which questions matter, and knowing when you've learned enough to act.

True experts immerse themselves. They get into the weeds. They simplify what others overcomplicate. And when the moment comes, they move decisively because they're prepared, not because they have a higher risk tolerance.

Warren Buffett is one of the best examples of this kind of expertise.

In 1963, a bizarre fraud involving salad oil nearly toppled one of America's most trusted companies. But it also gave Buffett one of the biggest opportunities of his career.

One of American Express' (Amex) subsidiaries guaranteed loans backed by what was supposed to be $150 million worth of soybean oil. In reality, Allied Crude Vegetable Oil Refining had filled giant storage tanks with seawater, then poured just enough salad oil on top to fool inspectors. When the scam collapsed, Amex stock dropped almost 50% in a matter of weeks. Newspapers speculated that the company's core business might go under as well.

While Wall Street panicked, Buffett studied. Many overlook the fact that Buffett isn't just a great investor, he's an expert in how businesses actually work. He's the type that prepares so thoroughly that he sees what others can't.

When asked how he spends his days, Buffett once said, "My job is basically reading." He reads hundreds of pages a day. As a kid, he read every investing book in the Omaha Public Library, most of them twice over. When studying a company, he reads annual reports going back decades, tracing decisions across different business cycles. He studies management behavior, incentives, and balance sheets. He doesn't look for opinions or hype, he seeks intimate understanding.

When Amex collapsed, Buffett didn't speculate or react. He dove into the details, studying their financial statements, old reports, history of similar cases, and the brand's competitive advantages. And then he did something no one else thought to do: he personally went to see how real people behaved.

One night at Ross's Steakhouse in Omaha, Buffett sat down at the table closest to the cashier for several hours. Customer after customer pulled out an Amex card to pay their bill. It was clear that the average American was unconcerned and largely unaware of the salad oil scandal. Buffett didn't need a spreadsheet to tell him what he was seeing. Amex hadn't lost trust. The brand was intact, its customers were loyal, and its core business was still strong.

Buffett refused to view the crisis through a single lens. He analyzed the balance sheet like an accountant, the brand like a marketer, and customer behavior like a psychologist. Expertise, for Buffett, wasn't depth in one discipline, it was fluency across many. Expertise is assembled, not inherited.

Buffett decided to invest $13 million (more than 40% of his partnership's capital at the time), acquiring 5% of the company while everyone else was running away. Within three years, his investment had tripled.

To some, the homerun Amex investment looked like luck. In reality, it was the predictable result of getting into the weeds. Doing the work others wouldn't, allowed Buffett to see what others couldn't. He'd trained himself to see what mattered. Though it appeared bold to many, the decision was obvious to someone who had done the work.

Buffett once said: "I don't look to jump over 7-foot bars; I look for 1-foot bars I can step over." His expertise is what makes those 1-foot bars visible.

This pattern of deep preparation, followed by decisive action, appears again and again throughout his career.

At age twenty, he took a train to GEICO's headquarters and spent several hours grilling their future CEO, Lorimer Davidson, on loss ratios, how the company calculated risk, and its cost structure. Most investors saw the company as a niche insurance agency. Buffett saw a fundamentally misunderstood business model with enormous upside. He invested three separate times over four decades. GEICO eventually became one of the defining investments inside Berkshire Hathaway, Buffett's holding company.

He would make the same type of bet again years later. In the early 1970s, the Washington Post Company was selling for roughly $100 million, despite owning assets worth several times that. Buffett had studied the business for years, so when regulatory fear drove the stock down, he bought 10% of the company for $10 million. That investment eventually grew to over $1.5 billion.

Buffett explains this kind of decision-making with an analogy: "You don't need to know a woman's exact age to know she's old enough to vote." If a business is clearly worth $500 million and selling for $100 million, you don't need perfect math. You need expertise that comes from years of studying how businesses actually behave. The work creates clarity. And clarity makes decisiveness possible. Experts don't need perfect information, they need sufficient understanding.

Though Buffett undoubtedly has great instincts, it's his preparation, discipline, and obsession with the craft that set him apart. He earns conviction by doing the work others skip.

Rather than waiting for certainty, the best leaders prepare so thoroughly that certainty becomes unnecessary. Preparation sharpens perception. In any field, whether investing, leadership, or combat, those who immerse themselves in their craft earn the right to act while others deliberate.

Section Three

The People

CARVE OUT

Fire and Forget

Two of the primary anti-tank missile systems used by U.S. Army ground forces are the TOW (Tube-launched, Optically tracked, Wire-guided) and the Javelin.

The TOW missile is wire-guided. Once fired, the operator must maintain line-of-sight and keep the target in the crosshairs until impact. While it's an effective weapon, this system exposes the operator to enemy fire and introduces opportunities for human error under stress. Early versions of the TOW also had operational limitations. For example, firing over water could degrade guidance performance due to wire drag and signal interference.

The Javelin works differently. It is a true "fire-and-forget" system. Once the operator locks onto a target and launches, the missile's onboard guidance takes over, homing in autonomously. The operator is free to take cover, reposition, or engage other targets, reducing exposure and increasing flexibility.

Teams are no different. Some people operate like TOW missiles, requiring constant guidance from launch to task completion. The best teams are built around Javelins – people who, once given clear intent and a defined target, can be trusted to execute on their own. Find those "fire and forget" people.

Point them in the right direction. Then let them fly.

CHAPTER 8

The Right People

"It doesn't make sense to hire smart people and then tell them what to do; we hire smart people so they can tell us what to do."

- STEVE JOBS

$1 + 1 \neq 2$

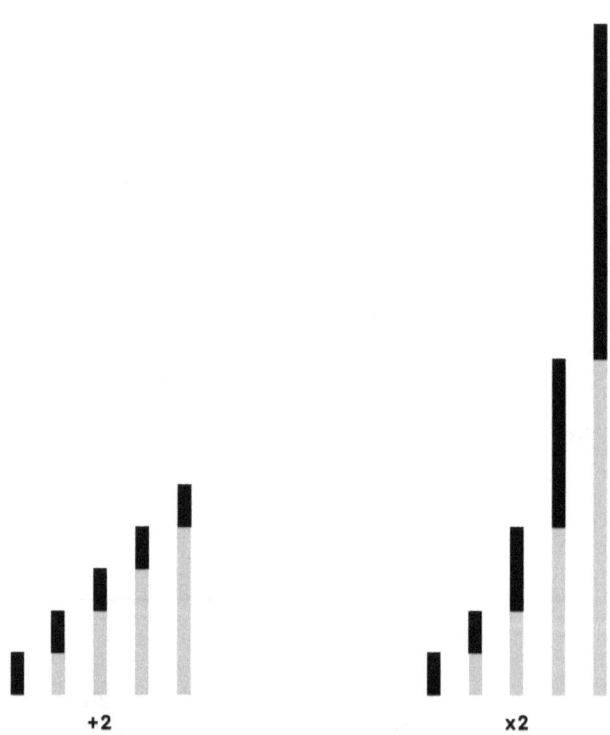

ADDITION VS. MULTIPLICATION

The <u>Right</u> People

By the early 1990s, the most iconic technology company in the world, IBM, was on the verge of collapse. This was the same company that invented the mainframe computer, dominated global technology, and once represented the very peak of American corporate excellence. But by 1993, IBM was bleeding out. Revenue had fallen from $69 billion to $57 billion and the company posted an astonishing $8.1 billion loss, the largest in U.S. corporate history at the time. Analysts predicted bankruptcy. Many believed IBM's only hope was to be broken into pieces and sold off for parts.

Inside, the view was even worse. IBM had become a giant maze where each group acted like its own kingdom. There were 266 separate general ledger systems, 29 different payroll systems, and the company was working with more than 70 various advertising agencies. The hardware, software, and services divisions all competed against each other for budget, relevance, and credit.

IBM didn't lack talent. It had world-class engineers, scientists, marketers, and operators. But over time, many had grown complacent inside a culture that valued consensus over initiative. The organization optimized for protecting turf instead of solving customer problems.

IBM had reached an inflection point. To survive, they didn't need a better strategy; they needed the right person to lead.

With the right people, the whole becomes far greater than the sum of its parts. Often, orders of magnitude greater. The right people challenge assumptions, see problems clearly, take ownership, and bring the courage to do things differently. Sometimes, they may even be industry outsiders.

That's exactly why IBM hired Louis V. Gerstner Jr. in 1993 – an executive who had never spent a single day in the computer industry. Having previously worked at American Express and McKinsey, Gerstner had most recently served as the Chairman and CEO of RJR Nabisco, a consumer goods company known for their popular cookie and cigarette brands. Not exactly the standard pipeline for running a tech giant. Critics were quick to point out that he wasn't an engineer and didn't understand technology deeply enough to fix IBM.

But that misunderstanding was exactly the point. IBM didn't need another engineer. They already had the best in the world.

What IBM needed was someone who could see the organization clearly, without the blinders of tradition or the weight of "how things have always been done."

"The last thing IBM needs right now is a vision," Gerstner famously said.

Gerstner arrived and immediately saw what insiders could not: the issue wasn't strategy. IBM had filing cabinets full of visionary documents correctly predicting every major technological shift over the years. The issue was execution. The company needed a culture shift that would bring out the best in their people and attract new ideas. They had a people crisis, not a technology crisis, bred by an overall lack of curiosity, urgency, and accountability.

Because of his time at RJR Nabisco, a company known for products like Oreo and Chips Ahoy, some people inside IBM nicknamed Gerstner the "Cookie Monster." Apparently, they were less than enthusiastic about the tough decisions he had to make in changing the culture. But what the Cookie Monster found was a company eating itself. They needed drastic changes before it was too late.

Gerstner began by stripping away the structural pieces that had calcified IBM. He forced functional teams to work together instead of against each other. He demanded candor, speed, and direct communication, making decisions in weeks that previously took years.

He centralized strategy, decentralized execution, and empowered the people who were closest to the work to act with speed and autonomy. He told managers that he welcomed mistakes, so long as they were made because someone moved too fast, not because they were paralyzed by caution or complacency. They wanted people with a bias for action, decreasing the time between thinking about something and doing something about it.

Above all, Gerstner focused relentlessly on the "who." He hired, elevated, and empowered people who were curious, hungry, and unafraid to challenge sacred assumptions.

Nowhere was this clearer than in marketing.

IBM's brand had become incoherent. Each division had hired its own advertising agency. There were over 70 different firms, each producing its own ads, taglines, visuals, and even different versions of the IBM logo.

Gerstner described it as, "Seventy tiny trumpets all tooting simultaneously for attention."

It was chaos. Without a unified message and no clear brand, there was no sense of IBM as a single entity. Until Gerstner recruited Abby Kohnstamm, an outsider, to lead marketing.

Kohnstamm wasn't a lifetime IBMer. She didn't grow up inside the engineering-first culture. She saw the company not as a collection of silos, but as a single global brand that desperately needed coherence. Her first major move was decisive: she eliminated all 70 agencies and consolidated IBM's brand under one – Ogilvy & Mather.

The result was the "Solutions for a Small Planet" campaign, a global rebrand that repositioned IBM from a hardware seller into a problem-solving partner for the digital age. It worked. Customers understood IBM again. Employees regained pride in the brand. For the first time in years, the message was clear, unified, and effective.

Kohnstamm embodied the type of person Gerstner believed could save IBM: curious, creative, and unafraid to take ownership. She wasn't limited by industry orthodoxy. And she didn't come from the culture, which is exactly what the culture needed.

With marketing turning the corner, Gerstner redirected his attention to another issue. One of the defining problems inside IBM was that executives had stopped listening to customers. Some hadn't visited a client site in years. Others didn't touch the product they were responsible for. As a response, Gerstner introduced "Operation Bear Hug," one of the boldest cultural resets in corporate history.

He ordered the top 50 executives (and later the top 100) to each visit at least five major customers within a two-month period. They were not allowed to send deputies, no scripts, and no presentations. They could only ask questions and listen. After each visit, executives were required to submit a four-page memo directly to Gerstner himself, and he read every one of them.

Some leaders discovered customers were furious: at pricing, at slow service, at disjointed product lines. Others discovered customers loved IBM's people but hated the fragmentation and internal turf wars. A few discovered that customers were ready to walk away entirely.

The message hit home. You can't lead people you don't talk to. You can't solve problems you don't see. And you can't transform a company from a conference room.

Operation Bear Hug forced leaders to confront reality. More importantly, it revealed the right *kinds* of people: those who were curious, willing to learn, eager to solve problems, and honest enough to face the truth. These were the leaders IBM would keep, promote, and empower.

Gerstner didn't singlehandedly save IBM. He saved it by finding the right people and giving them the room to operate.

The results speak for themselves. From 1994 to 1998, IBM generated $9.5 billion in cost savings. Hardware development cycles dropped from four years to sixteen months, and services revenue more than tripled. The company returned to profitability in 1994 and regained global relevance.

But the deeper victory was cultural. IBM learned how to be curious again. How to move fast again. How to think like problem-solvers, and how to let go of the past and build for the future.

Great organizations aren't rescued by plans alone. They're transformed by the right people. People who question assumptions, take ownership, and refuse to do things the way they've always been done. When you get the right people on board, *one plus one becomes far more than two.*

▼

First Who, Then What

Jim Collins coined the phrase "first who, then what" after studying successful businesses in his book, *Good to Great.* He concluded that before you decide where you're going, you must first decide who is going with you. For any team, getting the right people on the bus and in the right seats matters more than having a perfectly defined destination.

Bill Walsh seemed to understand this principle implicitly when he took control of the San Francisco 49ers in 1979. He knew that a complete overhaul of the organization was necessary to reach his Standard of Performance. When he first walked in the door, all he could see was disorder. There was a lack of pride from the front office all the way down to the players.

Bill's predecessor, Joe Thomas, had attempted to reinvent the franchise by stripping headquarters of trophies and past accomplishments. He also mortgaged the team's future by trading away valuable draft capital for an aging running back named O.J. Simpson. Thomas hoped "The Juice" would bring enough fanfare to fill the seats at Candlestick Park. Instead, injuries sidelined Simpson and the team languished.

For a brief moment in his first season, Bill tried similar promotional efforts to fill the stands, but every strategy failed. He quickly learned that no amount of marketing can energize a fan base. *Build a winner, and the fans will come.*

At the time, there was no connection to the past, pride in the present, or hope for the future. Players dragged through practices, taking frequent breaks to sit on their team-issued helmets. The practice field wasn't even 100 yards long, and coaches shouted through paper-thin walls in cramped meeting rooms. Nothing about the organization resembled a championship operation.

Bill said, "It takes talented athletes as well as an efficient organization to win games and championships."

Step one was building that organization, which started with hiring the right people.

Hiring is a challenge for every leader. Job descriptions and interview questions can become so cumbersome that it's easy to lose sight of what actually matters.

Warren Buffett famously distilled hiring down to three traits: "In looking for people to hire, you look for three qualities: integrity, intelligence, and energy. And if you don't have the first, the other two will kill you. If you hire somebody without [integrity], you really want them to be dumb and lazy, not intelligent and energetic."

Independent of each other, Bill and Buffett arrived at nearly identical criteria. *Integrity, Intelligence, and Energy.*

Integrity

Bill understood the reality of rebuilding an NFL franchise. They would face constant pressure and unrelenting scrutiny. He needed people whose character he could count on. Not when times were good, but when everything was on the line. Highly competitive environments reveal true character. Some people fold under the pressure, and others rise to the challenge. If Bill hired you, he needed to trust you.

Intelligence

Next, Bill looked for what he called functional intelligence. "One person who is not very bright but very aggressive in pushing his ideas can destroy an organization," he warned. He wanted people who could adapt as the game evolved, not those who were trapped in outdated assumptions. He told his coaches, "Set aside your ego. Be more concerned with finding the right way than in having it your way." The goal was to find better answers, not to win arguments.

Energy

Finally, Bill sought people who were "enthusiastic, inquisitive, and who would thrive on the work." He wanted to surround himself with coaches who genuinely loved the game and were passionate about mastering their craft. He said, "The gratification [a coach] gets from their work should come from their day-to-day involvement, the process itself, and not so much from reaching a titled position with high visibility. The means itself should be more important than the ends." In other words: do you love what you do, or do you love what it does for you? Energy and enthusiasm should stem from devotion to the process, not the promise of recognition.

Once Bill assembled a staff with integrity, intelligence, and energy, he eliminated silos. The 49ers became a cohesive organization, sharing information freely and searching for solutions together. Coaches and scouts worked side by side to identify and acquire talent, constantly refining their approach in search of a winning edge.

But coaches and scouts can't take snaps on Sunday. As legendary Alabama coach Paul "Bear" Bryant used to say, "No coach has ever won a game by what he knows; it's what his players know that counts."

Bill was determined to bring in the right players to execute his system. It would be the players' athleticism and execution that would make his ideas come to life.

In his second season as head coach, the 49ers disappointingly finished 6-10, but there were signs of progress. His offense had become one of the league's best passing attacks, but the defense was a disaster. Their secondary couldn't stop anyone. While they had one of the best passing offenses in football, they also had one of the *worst* passing defenses.

When reflecting on the 1980 season, Bill said, "Nothing is quite so discouraging to a team as knowing no lead is safe because the other team can score so quickly through the air." Each week at practice, the 49ers had a revolving door of defensive backs work out for the team, desperately trying to address their glaring weakness. While most players had their name inscribed on a piece of tape on their helmet, the equipment staff stopped giving name-tags to the new players because they would be there for a day and cut the next. The situation was dire, and Bill addressed it decisively.

In the following draft, the 49ers selected defensive players with six of their first seven picks. They took cornerback Ronnie Lott in the first round, cornerback Eric Wright in the second, and safety Carlton Williamson in the third. This type of draft strategy was unheard of at the time. Most teams spread their draft capital across multiple positions, but Bill concentrated all of his resources where it mattered most. One thing was certain: if Bill saw a problem, he attacked it.

In training camp before the following season, Bill tasked his coaching staff with preparing three rookies to start in the secondary for Week One. Coaches George Seifert and Ray Rhodes worked tirelessly with the young players to get them prepared. They had them arrive early and stay late. Seifert even ran the young players through the nearby neighborhood to ensure their conditioning was up to par.

Bill's gamble paid off. Rookie Ronnie Lott was named to the Pro Bowl, and the other young defensive backs performed well. The rebuilt secondary, paired with their dynamic offense, propelled the 49ers to a Super Bowl victory in the 1981-82 season.

Lott's impact extended far beyond his play on Sundays. He entered the league under the mentorship of Jack "Hacksaw" Reynolds, the veteran linebacker known for his intensity, preparation, and relentless standards. As discussed in the Introduction, Hacksaw was "the right kind of crazy," which is simply another way of saying obsessed. He modeled habits that couldn't be coached into existence: showing up early, taking exhaustive notes, and treating preparation as a daily discipline. Those habits took root in Lott, shaping the foundation of a Hall of Fame career. Before long, Lott's obsession began to spread throughout the locker room.

Bill said, "When you bring a 'Ronnie Lott' into your organization, you are actually bringing several 'Ronnie Lotts' aboard, because they create others in their own image. [They attract] teammates who share that same work ethic, intensity, and enthusiasm." Bill didn't need to motivate players like that; their drive was intrinsic. His job was to build a structure strong enough to support them and clear enough to let them lead.

Steve Jobs described the same dynamic while building Apple:

"I've built a lot of my success on finding these truly gifted people, and not settling for "B" and "C" players, but really going for the "A" players. I found that when you get enough "A" players together, when you go through the incredible work to find these "A" players, they really like working with each other. Because most have never had the chance to do that before. And they simply don't work with "B" and "C" players, so it's self-policing. They only want to hire "A" players. So you build these pockets of "A" players, and it just propagates."

Great leaders create an environment for obsession to thrive. They invite their people to dream big and dare greatly. Excellence attracts excellence and high standards repel mediocrity. When the right people arrive, they raise the bar for everyone else.

> *"Mediocre people don't like high achievers, and high achievers don't like mediocre people. So if everybody doesn't buy-in to the same principles and values of the organization at the same high standard, you're never going to be successful."*
>
> **- NICK SABAN**

There are countless examples of Bill getting the right people on the bus.

Joe Montana was a slender quarterback overlooked by many NFL scouts who doubted he could handle the punishment from professional defenses. But he was the perfect fit for Bill's West Coast Offense. His graceful footwork and pinpoint accuracy became the gold standard of quarterback play, ending his Hall of Fame career with a 63 percent completion rate.

Jerry Rice may have been the clearest expression of Bill's eye for people. Rice came from tiny Mississippi Valley State and doubted he'd even be drafted. Though he was a record-setting wide receiver for Archie "Gunslinger" Cooley in the Satellite Express Offense, he was prepared for a career in electronics repair if he didn't make it to the NFL. The night before a Sunday game, watching college football in his hotel room, Bill fell in love with the dynamic wide receiver. He had to have him.

Later picked in the first round by the 49ers, Rice

became the greatest wide receiver in the history of football. His 1,549 catches for 22,895 yards and 197 touchdowns are records that may never be broken. He transformed Bill's offense from a methodical, ball-control attack into a quick-strike, high-octane system that defined an entire decade of the NFL.

Bill had a gift for spotting under-the-radar talent. But he also had an uncanny ability to identify force multipliers—people whose character, leadership, and work ethic elevated everyone around them.

Lott, Montana, and Rice were exceptional players, but more importantly, they reflected the culture Bill was building. He knew that *great people do more than simply fit into a system, they define it.* Once they set the standard, everything else rises to meet it.

▼

The Wright Brothers and the Magic Third Guy

In December 1903, the world saw something it had never seen before: a machine, heavier than air, lifting a human being into the sky under its own power. Though it looked like magic at the time, it was the predictable result of having the right people on a mission that demanded obsession, creativity, and ownership at every level.

The Wright Brothers weren't well-funded scientists or credentialed engineers. They were bicycle mechanics from Dayton, Ohio. They had no formal training in aeronautics, physics, or mechanical engineering. What they *did* have was the rarest resource of all: insatiable curiosity and an obsession with figuring things out.

The brothers also had an extreme bias for action, and naturally attracted others who were the same. These people were "fire and forget," capable of carrying out a mission with little direction or oversight. Their story is one of the greatest examples of how the right people, not credentials or resources, achieve the impossible.

In the late 1890s and early 1900s, many prominent scientists were racing to be the first in flight. European governments funded enormous research labs. The U.S. government spent $70,000 (roughly $2 million today) on Samuel Langley's "Great Aerodrome," built by elite engineers from the Smithsonian.

Meanwhile, the Wright Brothers only spent around $1,000 over many years of experimentation, funded entirely by their bike shop. And yet it was the bicycle mechanics who cracked the code.

They were obsessed. They read every aeronautical publication they could find in English, French, or German. They built wind tunnels in their shop and tested more than 200 different wing designs. They taught themselves control systems, aerodynamics, and propeller theory. They even built their own tools, pursuing their craft with the intensity of people who couldn't imagine doing anything else.

By 1903, the Wrights had solved two of the three great problems of flight: lift and control. The final challenge was propulsion. They needed a lightweight engine powerful enough to get them off the ground. Every manufacturer they approached told them their idea was impossible. Engines were far too heavy, and if flight was doable, Langley's massive government-funded project would have figured it out already.

So instead of searching for the right backer, they found the right person. They turned to the quiet, soft-spoken mechanic who worked in the back of their bicycle shop: Charles E. Taylor.

Taylor wasn't an engineer, and he had never designed an engine before. Still, without proper instruction manuals, blueprints, or reference models, he promised to give it a shot. What followed was one of the most remarkable bursts of inventive brilliance in American history.

Taylor designed the engine from scratch, even fabricating many of the tools he needed. At a time when most engines were made of heavy cast iron, he figured out how to cast the crankcase in aluminum. The Wright Brothers told him the engine could weigh no more than 200 pounds and needed to produce at least eight horsepower. Taylor delivered a model that weighed just 179 pounds and produced twelve horsepower.

Even more astonishing, while most engines of the era required months of tuning, Taylor's ran on its second attempt. And he accomplished all of that in only six weeks.

This is the multiplier effect of the right person. They don't require hand-holding or micromanagement. And when they're truly "fire and forget," sometimes, when given an impossible mission, they bring back a miracle.

On December 17, 1903, everything finally converged. Years of obsessive research, dozens of failed tests, a relentless bias for action, and Charlie Taylor's engine. The flyer lifted off the dunes of Kill Devil Hills and carried Orville Wright for twelve seconds, covering 120 feet. The next flight carried Wilbur nearly 900 feet.

Orville later said that the Wright Brothers could not have flown without Charlie Taylor.

History didn't change because the Wright Brothers had the most money, the best credentials, or the backing of powerful institutions. It changed because they had the right person. Someone obsessed with his craft, willing to get his hands dirty, and armed with the courage to keep going.

The right person became the difference between another failed attempt and the first powered flight in human history.

In any endeavor worth pursuing, a small number of the right people will always outperform a crowd of the wrong ones.

CHAPTER 9

Fast and Flat

"Train people well enough so they can leave, treat them well enough so they don't want to."

- RICHARD BRANSON

"Don't tell people how to do things, tell them what to do and let them surprise you with their results."

- GEORGE S. PATTON

"Create a culture in which it is ok to make mistakes and unacceptable not to learn from them."

- RAY DALIO

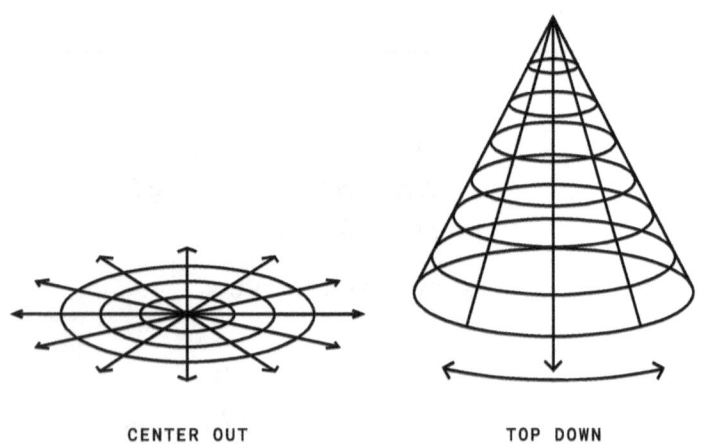

CENTER OUT   TOP DOWN

TEAM > HIERARCHY

On April 24, 1980, the United States launched Operation Eagle Claw, a daring attempt to rescue 52 American hostages held in Tehran. It ended in disaster.

In a remote Iranian desert refueling site known as Desert One, a helicopter collided with a C-130 transport aircraft loaded with fuel and U.S. Army Delta Force operators. Eight servicemembers were killed. The mission involved 44 aircraft, multiple ground vehicles, and elite units from the Army, Navy, Air Force, Marines, and intelligence agencies. Most of them had never trained together. Communications were spotty, responsibilities were fragmented, and decision-making was painfully slow for an operation that demanded speed and precision.

Eagle Claw exposed a brutal truth: America's most elite units were world-class individually, but structurally dysfunctional together. The U.S. needed a standing organization that could integrate the nation's most sensitive special operations units into a coherent, joint force. Joint Special Operations Command (JSOC) was created in 1980 as that answer.

For a time, JSOC's traditional hierarchy and tight compartmentalization made sense. It was built for sensitive, high-risk, carefully planned missions in a relatively slow-moving, non-digital world. But by the early 2000s, that world no longer existed.

When General Stanley McChrystal took command of JSOC in 2003, he inherited one of the most elite, capable, and technically proficient fighting forces in the world. But he also inherited an organization designed for a different era. It was hierarchical, siloed, and meticulously optimized for a more predictable enemy.

Terrorist networks like Al-Qaeda in Iraq (AQI) operated with a speed, decentralization, and adaptability that JSOC's traditional structure couldn't match. AQI was fluid, fast, and constantly reconfiguring. JSOC was a precise and powerful machine, but slow to adapt.

As McChrystal later described the start of his command: "We were losing to an enemy who, in conventional terms, shouldn't have stood a chance."

The problem wasn't talent. JSOC had the best people, but the organization wasn't letting those people be their best.

Before McChrystal, JSOC units (like SEAL Team Six, Delta Force, Army Rangers, and intelligence elements) operated as *tribes*. Each had its own compound, its own culture, and its own information pipeline. Operations that required integrated intelligence, surveillance, targeting, and ground assault were slowed by long approval chains, poor cross-unit communication, and junior leaders who were fearful of making decisions without senior sign-off.

The breakthrough came when analysts mapped AQI's structure and realized it wasn't a hierarchy at all, it was a living network. It behaved like a start-up, not a state. If JSOC wanted to win, it had to evolve from a machine into a network of teams that was fast, flat, transparent, and adaptive. It had to transform from a "tribe of tribes" into a "team of teams."

At first, McChrystal believed this would simply require tweaking strategy; "like changing offensive concepts partway through a football game," as he later put it. But as the fight unfolded, he realized how wrong that analogy was. He equated it more to switching from playing football to playing basketball. What JSOC needed wasn't a new playbook. It needed a new game entirely.

His core principles were:

1. Shared Consciousness

Information would no longer flow top-down or unit-to-unit. It would flow to everyone, constantly. He created a daily synchronized video teleconference (VTC) that spanned over 70 locations worldwide. Thousands of analysts, operators, and commanders received the same intelligence at the same time, eliminating blind spots.

2. Empowered Execution

Once people had context, they were given decision-making authority. McChrystal said, "If you want people to make good decisions, you have to give them the information they need – and then trust them."

This mirrors a principle popularized by Netflix: lead with context, not control. Leaders define the intent, establish clear boundaries, and then step back. In military terms, this is known as setting "left and right limits." In providing parameters without prescribing every move, teams are trusted to execute using their judgement, experience, and initiative.

3. Developing Leaders at Every Level

McChrystal intentionally developed junior leaders through access, not instruction. He regularly called front-line leaders to ask what they were seeing on the ground and how headquarters could remove obstacles.

His intention was to learn, not micromanage. To develop people and flatten the organization.

JSOC went from a siloed organization to the fastest-moving, most adaptive organization on earth. And nowhere was that more evident than in the hunt for Abu Musab al-Zarqawi.

At the time, Zarqawi was the most dangerous terrorist in Iraq, responsible for mass bombings, executions, and igniting sectarian civil war. Finding him required unimaginable speed, adaptability, and intelligence integration. JSOC's transformation made it possible.

Operations began to move at a relentless pace. A raid would generate intelligence, analysts processed it in real time, new targets were identified, and operators launched again almost immediately. What once took days now took hours. The feedback loop tightened, and Zarqawi's network began to collapse.

In the spring of 2006, JSOC pinpointed a meeting of suspected AQI leaders at a farmhouse in a rural area west of Baghdad. After a firefight, intelligence revealed additional insurgent activity nearby. The commanders on the ground pivoted instantly. A second raid followed, resulting in the capture of twelve men.

This was McChrystal's "fast and flat" organization in action.

Commanders had the authority to adjust in real time. Analysts had full visibility into operations and could prioritize what mattered most. Instead of climbing the hierarchy, information flowed across the network.

Weeks later, one of the detainees disclosed a critical detail during interrogation: Zarqawi met monthly with his spiritual advisor.

JSOC moved quickly, identifying the advisor, and placing him under constant surveillance. McChrystal called it "the unblinking eye."

When analysts observed the man relocate his family to a safehouse, they knew it was an indicator that a high-risk meeting was imminent. They followed him as he left Baghdad, switched vehicles, and drove north to Baqubah. Stopping at a restaurant, he switched vehicles again, and finally arrived at a nice house.

Zarqawi himself stepped outside to greet him.

Helicopters were dispatched immediately. Though the assault force was only twenty minutes away, helicopter maintenance issues delayed their flight. Waiting risked losing the target.

With an F-16 fighter jet already on station, the time-sensitive decision was made to execute an airstrike on Zarqawi's location. As McChrystal recounts, the commander "didn't ask my permission, and I didn't ask them to ask. I'd learned that trust was critical. Deviating from the modus operandi we had worked so hard to foster, even when the stakes were high, would be a mistake."

Two 500 pound bombs destroyed the house with Zarqawi inside. The most elusive terrorist in Iraq was eliminated.

This was a case study in leadership development at scale. Thousands of empowered leaders operated with the speed of one mind.

McChrystal's transformation wasn't about eliminating hierarchy. It was about developing people so thoroughly that hierarchy wasn't needed for every decision. He created a culture where leaders at all levels shared strategic understanding, decisions were made closest to the problem, and people operated with autonomy grounded in context.

McChrystal described the approach as, "Eyes on, hands off." Trust replaced micromanagement.

That philosophy transformed performance. JSOC increased the number of monthly raids from ten to 300, with minimal increases in personnel and funding. Even while moving exponentially faster, their raids were more successful, finding a higher percentage of their targets.

Great leaders don't just build better systems. They build better people.

In complex environments like war, business, and sports, the challenge isn't finding talent. It's enabling that talent to operate at its full potential. McChrystal rewired JSOC for speed. But more importantly, he rewired thousands of people for leadership.

▼

Control the Standard, Not the People

In 1987, the San Francisco 49ers traveled to New Orleans to face the Saints in the Louisiana Superdome. It was one of the loudest environments in football, and the deafening noise intimidated opposing coaches. Amid the roar of the crowd, the Saints' famed "Dome Patrol" defense had built a reputation for terrorizing quarterbacks, with outside linebackers Rickey Jackson and Pat Swilling piling up twenty sacks that season.

Despite the noise and pressure, Bill Walsh was confident in the game plan. At halftime, he reminded his team of a specific play he intended to call when they drove inside the 30-yard line.

In the second half, as the offense drove down the field, the noise of the Superdome and the intensity of the moment pulled Bill off script. He forgot to call the play they planned.

Backup quarterback Steve Young stepped in and reminded him. Bill listened, agreed, and on the next down, called the play, resulting in a 49ers touchdown.

What gets lost in this story is the remarkable selflessness and commitment to winning on both sides of that exchange. Young would go on to be a Hall of Fame quarterback. At the time, however, he was locked in a contentious quarterback controversy with another future Hall of Famer, Joe Montana. Young was confident in his abilities and believed he should be the starter. At times, he resented Bill for sticking with Montana. And yet, in that moment, he set ego aside and spoke up, reminding his coach of a play designed to help Montana succeed.

Bill could have ignored his backup quarterback, as many coaches would have. Instead, he listened. That only happens when trust has been built through shared preparation, open communication, and mutual respect.

That brief exchange captured something essential about the 49ers' culture. The team won that day (and many others) because trust mattered more than hierarchy.

In high-pressure situations, teams rise or fall to the level of trust they've built. Without trust, you don't stand a chance. Trust is not static. It must be cultivated through consistent, clear, and open communication. Trust requires leaders and teammates to set ego aside long enough to listen.

But trust alone isn't enough. Leadership still demands decisiveness. Highly effective leaders have a clear vision and the will to pursue it. Their clarity and confidence keep the team moving forward. But decisiveness carries a hidden risk. When leaders insist on being the final voice on every decision, their strength becomes a bottleneck. The unintended consequence is that their need for control causes everyone else in the organization to stand around waiting while they deliberate.

A *fast and flat* organization requires something different: a decisive leader who also empowers people to make decisions with confidence. They clear the way for their team to act quickly, without being burdened by unnecessary bureaucracy. Great leaders do more than make decisions, they build decision-makers.

> *"Bureaucracy is a construction by which a person is conveniently separated from the consequences of his or her actions."*
>
> **- NASSIM NICHOLAS TALEB**

When Bill took over as the head coach of the 49ers, he brought a clear vision for rebuilding the team and a Standard of Performance that held everyone accountable. He drafted detailed job descriptions for everyone in the organization. No role was too small. He even wanted the receptionists to answer the phone in a first-class manner. "If I had a word for

Bill," one of his former players recalled, "it would be *control.* It's almost impossible to think of him without it." And yet, control didn't mean micromanagement. "Once he hired them," one employee remembered, "Bill left them alone to do what needed to be done, however they chose to do it, but he expected them to deliver and let them know in no uncertain terms if they didn't."

Bill managed outcomes, not methods.

He proved that conviction and empowerment are not mutually exclusive. Bill held strong beliefs, but he wasn't rigid about how those beliefs were executed. "Success doesn't care which road you take to get to its doorstep," he said. Decisions were judged by results. Opinions evolved as new information emerged, and admitting error was an important part of the process, not a weakness. The goal was to win, and Bill's team was always looking for the winning edge.

That kind of excellence can only be achieved when everyone is committed to placing learning before ego. Hedge fund manager Ray Dalio calls it an "idea meritocracy" – the best idea wins, no matter where it comes from. But such an environment doesn't happen by accident. It starts with the leader. Do you model your own high standard? Can you demand excellence while still giving people the freedom to do their best work?

As author David Harris observed, "Walsh's first operational principle was that everyone in the organization had a role to play and needed to devote themselves to playing that role as well as they could. And while the organization had multiple roles, it had no strata. Everyone, big or small, was of import, equally deserving of respect and equally responsible for succeeding."

Bill believed that clarity breeds confidence. When people know their role, they can master the details that make teams great. He firmly believed that "championships are won with the bottom half of the roster." He didn't cater to top performers. He made sure everyone was valued for their contribution. One of his players remembered, "If you did your role well, he would recognize you for it. He would design plays for your skills." It didn't matter if you were the starting quarterback or a punt returner, Bill wanted each individual to become a superstar in *their* role.

The leader's job is to clearly define the role and then create space for their people to excel within it. That is how you truly develop people.

When leaders provide clarity of intent and freedom of execution, organizations move faster. Trust grows, and decisions flatten. They become fast and flat. People become accountable because they are trusted, not because they are controlled.

> ## "People don't care how much you know until they know how much you care."
> ### - ATTRIBUTED TO THEODORE ROOSEVELT

So how do you achieve this when ego inevitably shows up?

Bill had a unique definition of ego: "Being distracted by your own importance."

He felt that nothing destroyed a team faster than selfishness and distraction. There is enough external noise; great teams can't afford internal conflict. In a highly competitive arena, disagreements happen, but Bill never let them fester. He encouraged everyone to "reestablish communication" and get back to solving problems.

At its core, Bill believed development was relational. That the only way a team could overcome adversity and achieve championship-level success was because of the love they had for each other. Each player was an extension of their teammates.

In his Hall of Fame Speech, Bill explained it this way:

"Leadership is what we developed with the San Francisco 49ers, that each man was an extension of the other. When Joe Montana threw the ball, Randy Cross was the extension of him. When Freddie Soloman caught it he was an extension of Randy Cross, and when Randy Cross blocked he was an extension of Fred Dean who was the extension of Ronnie Lott who was the extension of Milt McCall so it was a chain link that was linked together by a group of men who learned to demand a lot of each other, to love each other, to care for each other to make any sacrifice for each other."

Individual accolades are the product of team success, and team success comes through collective sacrifice.

"We prepare for every contingency," Bill said, "and through all of this is a single thrust – sacrifice for your team because you infinitely care."

That is how talent is developed. Not through control or hierarchy. But through trust, communication, and shared responsibility.

▼

Radical Candor

Before Pixar became synonymous with near-flawless storytelling, it almost went bankrupt.

Through the late 1980s and early 1990s, Pixar wasn't a movie studio at all. It was a struggling hardware company selling high-end graphics computers (the "Pixar Image Computer"), losing money year after year. Steve Jobs kept the lights on only by writing checks totaling more than $50 million of his own money without any sign that the company would make it. They survived on odd jobs: animated commercials for Listerine and Tropicana, and a tiny research and development animation team making shorts that won awards but produced negligible revenue.

Pixar had unbelievably talented people. People like John Lasseter, Pete Docter, and Joe Ranft who would become legends in the film and animation world. But the company had not yet built the environment necessary to unlock that talent.

Early in the development of *Toy Story*, Pixar learned this the hard way. During a disastrous early cut known internally as the "Black Friday Reel," Woody had become an unlikable jerk due to forced creative changes from Disney executives. It was a painful lesson that false harmony, hierarchical interference, and a lack of honest critique could wreck a film.

This experience led to the creation of what became Pixar's most important innovation, one that was cultural rather than technological: the Braintrust.

The Braintrust wasn't made of the highest-ranking executives, it was a diverse group of Pixar's strongest storytellers who met regularly to critique works-in-progress and provide each movie director with feedback.

The rules for each meeting were clear:

Radical candor

Criticize the idea, not the person. No sugarcoating. No politics. No ego.

Notes, not mandates

The Braintrust had no authority to force changes. Directors remained fully in charge to implement or discard the ideas from the meetings.

Transparency over hierarchy

The truth mattered more than status.

Pixar co-founder Ed Catmull later wrote:

"The Braintrust is our most effective tool. Its hallmark is unvarnished candor. You are not your idea, and if you identify too closely with your ideas, you will take offense when they are challenged."

That principle formed the foundation that allowed Pixar to produce a string of unprecedented hits. Household classics like *Finding Nemo, Up, Inside Out*, and *Monsters, Inc.*

Catmull often summarized the concept bluntly, "All our movies suck at the beginning."

He wasn't being self-deprecating, he was expressing their developmental philosophy. At Pixar, the goal was never to avoid bad first drafts. It was to build a system where bad first drafts could be transformed into great films through candid collaboration. That system would be put to the ultimate test with *Toy Story 2*.

In 1998, *Toy Story 2* was in trouble. Disney, which owned the *Toy Story* sequel rights, originally intended the sequel to be a direct-to-video release. A small Pixar team developed an early version under severe time constraints, but when the Braintrust reviewed it, the verdict was bad:

"This movie doesn't work. It's not ready, and it can't be released like this."

Pixar made the radical decision to scrap most of the movie and rebuild the entire story from scratch. Through Herculean efforts across the team, they managed to pull it off in just eight months.

The pace nearly broke the team. Animators slept under their desks. People worked 70 to 80 hour weeks. At one point, a technical glitch accidentally deleted 90% of the film from Pixar's servers. The only reason it was saved was because Supervising Technical Director, Galyn Susman, who was working remotely while caring for her newborn, had a full backup at home.

Against impossible odds, Pixar delivered. The rebuilt *Toy Story 2* earned 100% on Rotten Tomatoes and became one of the most celebrated sequels ever made.

Yet the lasting win extended far beyond the box office. It was the system that turned pressure, failure, and feedback into growth.

More than creativity, Pixar's breakthrough was how they developed their people and created a culture where excellence could emerge. They made candor normal, not personal, teaching teams that feedback is a gift, not a threat.

The best ideas come from empowered people, not hierarchical control, and long-term growth must be prioritized over short-term comfort.

The Braintrust made more than great movies; it made world-class filmmakers.

> *"If you don't practice candor, you're not doing people a favor – you're robbing them of the chance to grow."*
>
> – ED CATMULL

Pixar transformed from a struggling hardware company into a creative force by doing one thing exceptionally well: They built a system where great people become even greater.

World-class organizations don't just hire talent. They develop it. And they create a culture where truth flows freely, decisions move quickly, and excellence is everyone's responsibility. *Fast and Flat.*

CHAPTER 10

Do Unto Others

"I've learned that people will forget what you said, people will forget what you did, but people will never forget how you made them feel."

- MAYA ANGELOU

"A leader is one who knows the way, goes the way, and shows the way."

- JOHN MAXWELL

YOU   TEAM   LEGACY

IT'S BIGGER THAN YOU

In January of 1976, Bill Walsh received an unexpected phone call.

He was anticipating a congratulatory message from his boss and mentor, Paul Brown. The Cincinnati Bengals had just finished an 11-3 season. Bill's quarterback, Ken Anderson, led the league in passing for the second straight year. After eight seasons serving under Brown and years spent refining what would become the West Coast Offense, Bill believed the next step was finally at hand: head coach.

Rumors had circulated for months that Brown was preparing to retire. Around the league, Bill was widely assumed to be the heir apparent.

Instead, when the phone rang that morning in January, it was a local columnist from *The Cincinnati Enquirer*. Bill was being asked for a comment because Brown had just retired, naming Bill "Tiger" Johnson the next head coach of the Bengals.

Bill sat in silence for nearly a minute. The reality was almost impossible to process. He had been passed over for a role he believed he had earned through years of innovation and loyal service. He would later describe it as the greatest disappointment of his life. Everything he had worked for seemed to crumble right before his eyes.

Devastated, Bill decided it was time for a change of scenery. "[I] felt it was time to look elsewhere if I was going to advance my career in the direction of eventually becoming a head coach," Bill recounted. He applied for offensive coordinator jobs around the league. Despite his success in Cincinnati, all he received was rejection.

In one interview, a team executive told him bluntly that Brown was sabotaging his job search. "The word going out on you isn't so good, Bill. People are hearing you're great with X's & O's, but you're not really a leader. Maybe that's why you're not getting offers." Bill felt a deep sense of betrayal.

"When it comes to deciding how you treat people," Bill said, "exploitation, expedience, and self-interest are a formula for creating a team of individuals who will soon be looking to join another team."

Not only was he passed over by the Bengals, but now his mentor was interfering with his ability to continue his career. Eventually, Bill landed a job with the San Diego Chargers. After one successful season, he was then offered the head coaching position at Stanford. Instead of standing in his way, Chargers head coach, Tommy Prothro, encouraged him to take the job. "For the good of your family and your career," Prothro told him, "go to Stanford!"

Bill never forgot that moment. He resolved that when he became a head coach, he would treat his assistants the way Prothro treated him. "While you are with us," Bill told his staff, "I expect you to give us everything you have. In turn, I will give you recognition and a chance to advance your own career."

True to his word, Bill helped his assistant coaches grow beyond him. In doing so, he built one of the most influential coaching trees in football history. By leading their own successful careers, his assistants multiplied his impact.

George Seifert won two Super Bowls as Walsh's successor in San Francisco. Mike Holmgren carried the West

Coast Offense to Green Bay and Seattle, building consistent winners. Andy Reid became one of the winningest coaches in NFL history. Jon Gruden and Steve Mariucci adapted Walsh's principles to new eras and new teams. Today, his imprint can be found across every NFL franchise.

Bill didn't cling to talent. He developed it and then let it go.

> *"Bill was blessed with one of the greatest gifts you can have, which is the ability to see the future potential of another human being."*
>
> **- STEVE YOUNG**

That choice reflected a deeper pattern in Bill's life that shows up across industries in every great leader. Legacy doesn't emerge all at once. It unfolds in stages, and each stage requires a different kind of courage.

1. The Courage to be yourself.

Early in your career, courage looks like authenticity. Every industry applies pressure to conform to the prevailing style, language, or playbook. It takes conviction to pursue your own vision instead of copying others. Bill showed this courage early, developing an offense that didn't resemble what football was "supposed" to look like.

2. The Courage to better yourself.

As you begin to experience success, a new test emerges. Early wins can be a false positive, tempting you to believe you've figured it out. Growth requires the humility to fight your ego, ignore the press clippings, and keep refining your craft. Bill never believed he had arrived. Even after Super Bowl victories, he remained relentless in his pursuit of improvement.

3. The Courage to lose yourself in love and service to others.

At the highest level, leadership demands a different kind of bravery—the willingness to make it no longer about you. To invest in others. To create opportunities, pass along hard-earned lessons, and take pride in seeing others surpass you. Legacy is built when leaders shift from chasing accomplishment to multiplying impact.

Bill is remembered not for the plays he called or all the wins he accumulated, but for the coaches and athletes he developed. His influence permeates every level of football.

As he famously said, "The four most powerful words are: I believe in you."

When discussing Bill, Joe Montana said, "His goal in life was to convince us that we could be great. And he did, and we were. That's why he was such a great leader."

The best leaders don't protect their position. They prepare their replacement. They don't diminish others to stay relevant. They elevate others to stay meaningful.

Great leadership is succession, not possession. The leader's ceiling becomes their people's floor. The true measure of success is how many others thank you for theirs.

Bring your own pencil and teach others to do the same. Then step back, and let them surpass you.

That is legacy.

KEEP ON GOING
— Bill Walton

Acknowledgements

I attended three high schools in three different states over the course of three years. In the midst of transition and being "the new kid," football became a constant. On the first day of school, I walked into class with 60 friends because I was on the football team.

My love for the game has only grown since then.

I learned through reading and studying that it was possible to "choose my own mentors." As I started coaching, I embraced Bill Walsh's wisdom, and his words became a guidepost for me.

I soon learned that Bill had also attended three high schools in three years. He also struggled to acclimate to new environments. He also found an anchor in football. I've felt a kinship ever since.

Over the past 5 years, I've read everything I can find by or about Bill, and I'm better for it.

Griff, thank you for taking on this project with me. We wrote "the book we would want to read." It is our life's work up to this point, but I know we will continue to grow.

One of my life philosophies is to do "long-term things with long-term people." I am fortunate to work on this project with the godparents of my kids and my forever family. Liz and Griff, thank you for the sacrifices you made to make our vision a reality.

To Grace, my partner in life and creativity. Thank you for bringing this project to life with your wisdom, patience, and design expertise. When I watch you master your craft, it inspires me to be better every day.

To Zion and Addie, you are the light of my life. Thank you for the hugs and unexpected interruptions that made the writing process infinitely more meaningful. I hope you both find your passion and build your life around it. I will be there to support you both every step of the way.

Bet on yourself and *keep going.*

DAN CASEY

A number of years ago, I happened to read *The Score Takes Care of Itself* and *Who Says Elephants Can't Dance?* at the same time. What struck me wasn't just that they were both turnaround stories, or that they unfolded during the same two-decade period. It was how remarkably similar the leadership and team-building philosophies of their central figures, Bill Walsh and Lou Gerstner, turned out to be.

Knowing Dan Casey loved Bill, I was eager to share what I had noticed. What I didn't know was that Dan had already been incubating an idea for a book on Bill, having made him a personal mentor over the years. I never could have imagined that our early conversations would lead to writing this book together.

Though our professional paths diverged since playing football together at Davidson College, what I've learned over time is that the same principles for success – Bill Walsh's Standard of Performance – apply across domains. What Dan saw produce greatness on the football field, I had seen generate the same outcomes in the military and in business. There's a blueprint, and it can be followed in any industry.

Dan, thank you for inviting me along on this journey. It's truly special to find a partner who operates on the same wavelength across an entire project. It's been uncanny to see how complementary our skills and perspectives are. Thank you for believing in me and trusting me from the very beginning, long before either of us could have imagined writing a book. It's an immense honor to see my name beside yours on this cover.

Grace, I remain genuinely amazed at your ability to take our amateur drawings and half-formed ideas and turn them into elegant works of art. This book quite literally came to life through your talent, and I'm convinced there is pure magic in what you do.

When I first mentioned this book to Joe Byerly, his immediate response was, "How can I help?" Joe, thank you for your sage advice, encouragement, invaluable connections, and for being an advocate from day one.

To my friends, mentors, and supporters, you have modeled many of the lessons in this book. Thank you for showing the way. Everywhere I look, I'm surrounded by examples of what "right" looks like. I'm beyond blessed to have such a crew.

Thank you to those who provided feedback on early drafts. Your perspectives and input meant more than you know.

There are so many stories that didn't make these pages. I'm deeply grateful to those who became my mentors through study, and whose lives and work continue to challenge me to live The Standard and pursue my own excellence.

To my family, thank you for setting the example from day one. There is no greater gift than your love and support. You laid the foundation, sparked my curiosity, and paved the way. Thank you for continuing to enthusiastically live life with us.

Kai, my greatest wish has always been that my ceiling becomes your floor. I hope the lessons distilled in this book prove helpful as you embark on your own wonderful journey. Thank you for always reminding me to play, and for your example of approaching each day with the utmost enthusiasm. Love always, Dad.

It's rare to find a life partner. Rarer still to find one who is a tremendous editor, tireless travel companion, and best friend. Lizzie, there aren't enough pages in the world to adequately thank you for what you mean to me. Thank you for being my sounding board, advisor, confidant, and partner in crime. As with everything else, you made this book possible in more ways than I can count. What a life we have lived together so far. May the road ahead be filled with endless adventure. I love you forever.

This book is ultimately about persevering, learning, and passing things on. I'm grateful to everyone who, over the years, has helped us do exactly that.

GRIFFIN BRAND

Bill Walsh's Standard of Performance

- Exhibit a ferocious and intelligently applied work ethic directed at continual improvement.
- Demonstrate respect for each person in the organization.
- Be deeply committed to learning and teaching.
- Be fair.
- Demonstrate character.
- Honor the direct connection between details and improvement; relentlessly seek the latter.
- Show self-control, especially where it counts most – under pressure.
- Demonstrate and prize loyalty.
- Use positive language and have a positive attitude.
- Take pride in my effort as an entity separate from the result of that effort.
- Be willing to go the extra distance for the organization.
- Deal appropriately with victory and defeat, adulation and humiliation.
- Promote internal communication that is both open and substantive.
- Seek poise in myself and those I lead.
- Put the team's welfare and priorities ahead of my own.
- Maintain an ongoing level of concentration and focus that is abnormally high.
- Make sacrifice and commitment the organization's trademark.

The Timeline

This book is built from stories that span teams, seasons, careers, and contexts. On their own, each moment carries weight. Together, they reveal something larger. This timeline gathers every story in one place to show how each is shaped by the same commitments: disciplined preparation, principled leadership, and the relentless pursuit of excellence.

1903:
- ▶ The Wright brothers achieve the first powered, controlled flight *(Ch. 8)*

1909:
- ▶ Theodore Roosevelt leaves office as President of the United States *(Ch. 4)*

1914:
- ▶ Ernest Shackleton begins the Imperial Trans-Antarctic Expedition *(Ch. 3)*
- ▶ Theodore Roosevelt embarks on the River of Doubt Expedition *(Ch. 4)*

1916:
- ▶ Shackleton completes the first overland crossing of South Georgia and rescues every member of his crew *(Ch. 3)*

1921:
- ▶ British expedition establishes an early Everest base camp on the north (Tibetan) side to scout routes *(Ch. 1)*

1948:
- ▶ John Wooden is named head coach of UCLA men's basketball *(Ch. 4)*

1951:
- ▶ Warren Buffet makes his first investment in GEICO while a college student *(Ch. 7)*

1953:

▹ The modern Everest Base Camp location on the Khumbu Glacier is established during John Hunt's expedition, leading to the first successful summit *(Ch. 1)*

1954:

▹ Coach Paul "Bear" Bryant leads the Texas A&M Aggies through a grueling training camp in Junction, Texas – an infamous lesson in overtraining *(Ch. 4)*

1955:

▹ Bill Walsh graduates from San Jose State and begins his coaching career as a graduate assistant under Bob Bronzan *(Ch. 2)*

1957:

▹ Bill Walsh hired as Head Coach at Washington Union High School in California *(Ch. 2)*

1960:

▹ Dr. Seuss' *Green Eggs and Ham* is published *(Ch. 6)*

1962:

▹ Phil Knight graduates from Stanford Business School and travels to Japan to explore importing running shoes *(Ch. 3)*

1964:

▹ Phil Knight and Bill Bowerman launch Blue Ribbon Sports *(Ch. 3)*

▹ John Wooden and UCLA win their first NCAA basketball championship *(Ch. 4)*

▹ Warren Buffett invests $13 million in American Express after the "Salad Oil Scandal" *(Ch. 7)*

1968:

▹ Bill Walsh becomes offensive coordinator for the Cincinnati Bengals *(Ch. 3)*

1969:

▹ Bengals quarterback Greg Cook is injured; Virgil Carter takes over, forcing Walsh to adapt, leading to the creation of the West Coast Offense *(Ch. 6)*

1971:

▶ Phil Knight's partnership with Onitsuka (Tiger) collapses *(Ch. 3)*

1972:

▶ Nike debuts its first shoe line at the U.S. Olympic Trials, with Steve Prefontaine as its rebel ambassador *(Ch. 3)*

1973:

▶ John Wooden is inducted into the Naismith Memorial Basketball Hall of Fame *(Ch. 4)*

▶ Warren Buffett acquires 10% of the Washington Post Company *(Ch. 7)*

1975:

▶ John Wooden wins his 10th NCAA championship at UCLA and announces his retirement *(Ch. 4)*

1976:

▶ Bill Walsh becomes offensive coordinator of the San Diego Chargers after being passed over in Cincinnati *(Ch. 3)*

▶ Commercial supersonic passenger service begins with the Concorde *(Ch. 5)*

▶ Berkshire Hathaway acquires a major stake in GEICO and Buffett joins the board *(Ch. 7)*

1977:

▶ Bill Walsh is named head coach at Stanford University *(Ch. 3)*

1978:

▶ James Dyson builds his first functional cyclone vacuum prototype *(Ch. 2)*

1979:

▶ Bill Walsh is hired by the San Francisco 49ers and drafts Joe Montana and Dwight Clark *(Ch. 3)*

▶ Bob Ladouceur begins coaching at De La Salle High School in the Bay Area *(Ch. 7)*

The Timeline

1980:

- Nike goes public with an IPO *(Ch. 3)*

- Operation Eagle Claw fails and Joint Special Operations Command (JSOC) is created *(Ch. 9)*

1982:

- Bill Walsh and 49ers win their first Super Bowl (1981 season) *(Ch. 3)*

1985:

- The 49ers finish their near perfect season and win their second Super Bowl under Bill Walsh (1984 season) *(Ch. 7)*

1989:

- The 49ers win their third Super Bowl under Walsh (1988 season) *(Ch. 4)*

- Bill Walsh steps down as head coach *(Ch. 4)*

1993:

- IBM hires Louis V. Gerstner Jr. as CEO *(Ch. 8)*

1995:

- Dyson becomes the best-selling vacuum brand in the UK *(Ch. 2)*

1996:

- Todd Graves opens the first Raising Cane's restaurant *(Ch. 6)*

- Berkshire Hathaway acquires the remainder of GEICO *(Ch. 7)*

1997:

- Reed Hastings is charged a $40 late fee at Blockbuster, sparking the idea for Netflix *(Ch. 5)*

1998:

- Sara Blakely develops the first Spanx prototype *(Ch. 2)*

- Netflix officially launches, receiving 137 orders on day one *(Ch. 5)*

- Dave Brailsford is hired by British Cycling as a consultant *(Ch. 7)*

1999:

- Pixar releases *Toy Story 2 (Ch. 9)*

2002:

- Elon Musk founds SpaceX and announces a long-term vision for Mars *(Ch. 5)*

2003:

- Supersonic transatlantic passenger flights are discontinued *(Ch. 5)*

2005:

- Paul Graham founds Y Combinator *(Ch. 2)*
- Hurricane Katrina devastates the Gulf Coast and Raising Cane's becomes the first major restaurant chain to reopen in affected areas *(Ch. 6)*

2006:

- JSOC eliminates Abu Musab al-Zarqawi using fast, decentralized operations *(Ch. 9)*
- SpaceX's first orbital launch attempt fails *(Ch. 5)*

2007:

- Netflix launches streaming video *(Ch. 5)*

2008:

- SpaceX successfully reaches orbit with Falcon 1 Flight 4 *(Ch. 5)*

2010:

- Blockbuster declares bankruptcy *(Ch. 5)*

2012:

- Sara Blakely becomes the youngest self-made female billionaire, according to *Forbes* *(Ch. 2)*

2019:

- U.S. Army Ranger medics conduct the first ROLO protocol in combat in Afghanistan *(Ch. 7)*

2025:

- Raising Cane's surpasses 900 locations, generating industry-leading revenue per store *(Ch. 6)*

POST GAME

Sources

Introduction | Bring Your Own Pencil

▷ **BOOKS**

Bryant, Paul "Bear," with John Underwood. Bear: *The Hard Life and Good Times of Alabama's Coach Bryant.* Little, Brown and Company, 1975.

Harris, David. *The Genius: How Bill Walsh Reinvented Football and Created an NFL Dynasty.* Random House Trade Paperbacks, 2008.

Lott, Ronnie, with Jill Lieber. *Total Impact: Straight Talk from Football's Hardest Hitter.* Doubleday, 1991.

Walsh, Bill, with Glenn Dickey. *Building a Champion: On Football and the Making of the 49ers.* St. Martin's, 1990.

Walsh, Bill, with Brian Billick and James A. Peterson. *Finding the Winning Edge.* Sports Publishing, 1998.

Walsh, Bill, with Steve Jamison and Craig Walsh. *The Score Takes Care of Itself: My Philosophy of Leadership.* Portfolio/Penguin, 2009.

▷ **ARTICLES AND DOCUMENTS**

Rovell, Darren. "Muhammad Ali's 10 Best Quotes," *ESPN*, June 3, 2016. https://www.espn.com/boxing/story/_/id/15930888/muhammad-ali-10-best-quotes.

Sturges, Paul Lt. Col. "10 Leadership Tips from 'The Bear'." *McConnell Air Force Base*, September 6, 2012. https://www.mcconnell.af.mil/News/Commentaries/Display/Article/225854/10-leadership-tips-from-the-bear/.

▷ **VIDEOS AND SPEAKING**

NFL Films. *America's Game: The 1981 San Francisco 49ers – Super Bowl XVI. Documentary.* NFL Films / NFL Network, 2006.

NFL Films. *America's Game: The 1984 San Francisco 49ers – Super Bowl XIX. Documentary.* NFL Films / NFL Network, 2006.

NFL Films. *America's Game: The 1989 San Francisco 49ers – Super Bowl XXIII. Documentary.* NFL Films / NFL Network, 2006.

A Note to the Reader

▷ **BOOKS**

Walsh, *The Score Takes Care of Itself.*

Carve Out: Military Radios

▶ ARTICLES AND DOCUMENTS

Harris Corporation. *Radio Communications in the Digital Age, Volume Two: VHF/UHF Technology.* First printing June 2000. PDF. Accessed January 5, 2026. https://www.trngcmd.marines.mil/Portals/207/Docs/TBS/RADIO%20COMMUNICATIONS%20VHF%20and%20UHF.pdf.

Chapter 1: Permanent Base Camp

▶ BOOKS

Daumal, René. *Mount Analogue: A Novel of Symbolically Authentic Non-Euclidean Adventures in Mountain Climbing.* Translated by Roger Shattuck. City Lights Books, 1959.

Krakauer, Jon. *Into Thin Air: A Personal Account of the Mt. Everest Disaster.* Doubleday, 1997.

Talty, John. T*he Leadership Secrets of Nick Saban: How Alabama's Coach Became the Greatest Ever.* Matt Holt Books, 2022.

Walsh, *The Score Takes Care of Itself.*

Wooden, John, and Steve Jamison. *Wooden: A Lifetime of Observations and Reflections On and Off the Court.* Contemporary Books, 1997.

▶ ARTICLES AND DOCUMENTS

Benjamin, Cody. "Inside Nick Sirianni's Unusual Eagles Meetings That Built Brotherhood." *Fox Sports,* February 4, 2025. https://www.foxsports.com/stories/nfl/inside-nick-siriannis-unusual-eagles-meetings-built-brotherhood.

Bold Himalaya. "Lukla to Everest Base Camp Trek: Distance & Duration." *Bold Himalaya,* November 9, 2025. https://boldhimalaya.com/lukla-to-everest-base-camp-trek-distance-duration/.

Places Nepal. "Distance from Everest Base Camp to the Summit of Mount Everest." *Places Nepal,* December 28, 2025. https://www.placesnepal.com/blog/distance-from-everest-base-camp-to-the-summit-of-mount-everest.

▶ VIDEOS AND SPEAKING

McVay, Sean. *Remarks at the University of Texas Coaching Clinic.* University of Texas, Austin, TX. Live lecture, March 22, 2024.

Carve Out: Into The Storm

▶ VIDEOS AND SPEAKING

Vaden, Rory. "Buffalo Charge the Storm Story by Rory Vaden." YouTube video, August 17, 2020. https://www.youtube.com/watch?v=azcS1SXoQeA&t=38s.

Chapter 2: Self-Belief Before Evidence

▶ BOOKS

Adams, Douglas. *The Hitchhiker's Guide to the Galaxy.* Pan Books, 1979.

Campbell, Joseph, with Phil Cousineau. *The Hero's Journey: Joseph Campbell on His Life and Work.* Harper & Row, 1990.

Dyson, James. *Invention: A Life of Learning Through Failure.* HarperCollins, 2021.

Dyson, James. *Against the Odds: An Autobiography.* Texere Publishing Limited, 1997.

Sources

Graham, Paul. *Hackers & Painters: Big Ideas from the Computer Age.* O'Reilly Media, 2004.

Harris, *The Genius.*

Walsh, *The Score Takes Care of Itself.*

▶ ARTICLES AND DOCUMENTS

Edison, Thomas A. Quoted in *Harper's Monthly Magazine,* September 1910 (paraphrased sentiment).

McCullough, David. Interview by Bruce Cole. "The Historian's Craft." *Humanities 23* (4) (July/August). National Endowment for the Humanities, 2002.

"Sara Blakely Profile." Forbes. Accessed January 5, 2026.https://www.forbes.com/profile/sara-blakely/?sh=4821264476bb.

"Thomas Edison Quotes." *Charles Edison Fund.* Accessed January 5, 2026. Walsh, Bill. "Flank Formation Football; Stress: Defense." Master's Theses, 9. 1958. https://scholarworks.sjsu.edu/etd_theses/9.

▶ INTERVIEWS AND PODCASTS

Ferriss, Tim. "#530 Sir James Dyson – Founder of Dyson and Master Inventor on How to Turn the Mundane into Magic." *The Tim Ferriss Show* (podcast episode), August 20, 2021. https://podcasts.apple.com/us/podcast/530-sir-james-dyson-founder-of-dyson-and-master/id863897795?i=1000534124244.

ForbesWomen. "Sara Blakely on the Origin Story of Spanx: 'I Was Just a Frustrated Consumer.'" YouTube video, November 3, 2021. https://www.youtube.com/watch?v=3hCtukSt_e0.

Raz, Guy. "Dyson: James Dyson (2018)." *How I Built This* (podcast episode), October 15, 2018. https://podcasts.apple.com/us/podcast/dyson-james-dyson-2018/id1150510297?i=1000445007913.

Raz, Guy. "Spanx: Sara Blakely." *How I Built This* (podcast episode), July 9, 2018. https://podcasts.apple.com/us/podcast/spanx-sara-blakely/id1150510297?i=1000396023160.

Robbins, Tony. "Sara Blakely: How She Built SPANX from the Ground Up." YouTube video, July 22, 2021. https://www.youtube.com/watch?v=BnvoO32JwP8.

Senra, David. "#300 James Dyson (Against the Odds)." *Founders* (podcast episode), June 15, 2023. https://open.spotify.com/episode/38bGUegp0jlk1jlGBWRnHz.

Stanford Graduate School of Business. "Sara Blakely, Founder and CEO, Spanx." YouTube video, April 17, 2018. https://www.youtube.com/watch?v=TPURpzGPMxQ.

Chapter 3: The Valley of Death

▶ BOOKS

Campbell, Joseph, with Bill Moyers. *The Power of Myth.* Doubleday, 1988.

Cohn, Lowell. *Rough Magic: Bill Walsh's Return to Stanford Football.* Simon & Schuster, 1994.

Collins, Jim. *Good to Great: Why Some Companies Make the Leap… and Others Don't.* HarperBusiness, 2001.

Glauber, Bob. *Guts and Genius: The Story of Three Unlikely Coaches Who Came to Dominate the NFL in the '80s.* Doubleday, 1989.

Harris, *The Genius.*

Horowitz, Ben. *The Hard Thing About Hard Things: Building a Business When There Are No Easy Answers.* HarperBusiness, 2014.

Kelly, Kevin. *Excellent Advice for Living: Wisdom I Wish I'd Known Earlier.* Portfolio/Penguin, 2023.

Knight, Phil. *Shoe Dog: A Memoir by the Creator of Nike.* Scribner, 2016.

Lansing, Alfred. *Endurance: Shackleton's Incredible Voyage.* McGraw-Hill, 1959.

Pressfield, Steven. *Gates of Fire: An Epic Novel of the Battle of Thermopylae.* Doubleday, 1998.

Walsh, *Building a Champion.*

Walsh, *Finding the Winning Edge.*

Walsh, *The Score Takes Care of Itself.*

> ### ARTICLES AND DOCUMENTS

Singh, Muskan. "Quote of the Day by Sigmund Freud: Top quotes by the father of psychoanalysis." *The Economic Times,* December 29, 2025. https://economictimes.indiatimes.com/news/international/us/quote-of-the-day-today-december-29-quote-of-the-day-by-sigmund-freud-one-day-in-retrospect-inspiring-quotes-by-the-father-of-psychoanalysis/articleshow/126231811.cms?from=mdr.

Stanhope, Philip Dormer, 4th Earl of Chesterfield. Letter to his son, November 6, 1747. In *Letters to His Son*, edited by Lord Mahon. London: John Murray.

Walsh, "Flank Formation Football; Stress: Defense."

> ### VIDEOS AND SPEAKING

"1980 Week 11 San Francisco 49ers at Miami Dolphins." YouTube video, uploaded by MJSIII, July 27, 2024. https://www.youtube.com/watch?v=KtxaTVowDRs.

"Naval Ravikant EXPOSES Why No One Can Beat You At Being You." YouTube short video, uploaded by WealthClipsVault, Dec. 27, 2025. https://www.youtube.com/shorts/pDjNW e8Iq7g.

> ### INTERVIEWS AND PODCASTS

Breen, Matt. "Ernest Shackleton." *The Explorers Podcast* (podcast episodes), May 28, 2021. https://explorerspodcast.com/ernest-shackleton/.

Chavez, Chris. "Nike Founder Phil Knight on Legacy and His Perspective on the Track and Field's Present State and Future." *The CITIUS MAG Podcast* (podcast episode), July 21, 2021. https://podcasts.apple.com/us/podcast/nike-founder-phil-knight-on-legacy-and-his/id1204506559?i=1000529585089.

Hutcheson, Stig. "TIP 096: Billionaire Phil Knight & Nike." *We Study Billionaires* (podcast episode), July 24, 2016. https://open.spotify.comepisode/572okjjcrDWNobFVVy5gM9.

Senra, David. "144 Ernest Shackleton." *Founders* (podcast episode), July 29, 2019. https://podcasts.apple.com/us/podcast/144-ernest-shackleton/id1141877104?i=1000529123960

Senra, David. "#186 Phil Knight (Nike)." *Founders* (podcast episode), June 16, 2021. https://open.spotify.com/episode/7oAXZchE3BAljEUmSr9sj4.

Wilson, Ben. "Nike Founder Phil Knight: How to Take Over the World." *How to Take Over the World* (podcast episode), August 6, 2024. https://podcasts.apple.com/us/podcast/nike-founder-phil-knight/id1333158713?i=1000664537983.

Chapter 4: Don't Quit a Hit Show

> ### BOOKS

Bryant, *Bear.*

Cohen, Rich. *The Fish That Ate the Whale: The Life and Times of America's Banana King.* Farrar, Straus and Giroux, 2012.

Dent, Jim. *The Junction Boys: How Ten Days in Hell with Bear Bryant Forged a Champion Team.* St. Martin's Press, 1999.

Sources

Fellowship of Christian Athletes. *The Greatest Coach Ever: Timeless Wisdom and Insights of John Wooden*. The Heart of a Coach Series. Fellowship of Christian Athletes, 2010.

Glauber, *Guts and Genius*.

Harris, *The Genius*.

Knight, *Shoe Dog*.

Millard, Candice. *The River of Doubt: Theodore Roosevelt's Darkest Journey*. Doubleday, 2005.

Sinek, Simon. *The Infinite Game*. Portfolio/Penguin, 2019.

Stevenson, Robert Louis. "El Dorado." In *The Complete Poetical Works of Robert Louis Stevenson*, 112. Chatto & Windus, 1903.

Stulberg, Brad, and Steve Magness. *Peak Performance: Elevate Your Game, Avoid Burnout, and Thrive with the New Science of Success*. Rodale Books, 2017.

Sullivan, Dan, and Dr. Benjamin Hardy. *The Gap and the Gain: The High Achievers' Guide to Happiness, Confidence, and Success*. Hay House, Inc., 2021.

Sullivan, Dan, and Dr. Benjamin Hardy. *Who Not How: The Formula to Achieve Bigger Goals Through Accelerating Teamwork*. Hay House, Inc., 2020.

Thoreau, Henry David. *Walden; or, Life in the Woods*. Ticknor and Fields, 1854.

Walsh, *The Score Takes Care of Itself*.

Wooden and Jamison, *Wooden*.

▶ ARTICLES AND DOCUMENTS

Impelman, Craig. "John Wooden's 7-Point Creed: 'Be True to Yourself.'" *TheWoodenEffect. com*, December 13, 2016. https://www.thewoodeneffect.com/john-woodens- 7-point-creed-true/.

Inskeep, Steve. "Tracing Roosevelt's Path Down the 'River of Doubt'." *NPR*, November 3, 2005. https://www.npr.org/2005/11/03/4986859/tracing-roosevelts-path-down-the-river-of-doubt.

"John Wooden." *Britannica*. Encyclopædia Britannica, Inc. Accessed January 6, 2026. https://www.britannica.com/biography/John-Wooden.

Lasley, Kevin R., and Alvin K. Benson. "John Wooden." *EBSCO Research Starters*, 2023. https://www.ebsco.com/research-starters/biography/john-wooden.

Story, Mark. "Wooden Started Coaching in Kentucky, and Lost." *Kentucky.com*, June 21, 2010. https://www.kentucky.com/sports/high-school/article44035443.html.

"The Health of Theodore Roosevelt." *Theodore Roosevelt Association Journal*. Library of Congress Manuscript Division. Theodore Roosevelt Digital Library. Accessed January 6, 2026. https://www.theodorerooseveltcenter.org/digital-library/o305933/.

"The Pyramid of SUCCESS." *TheWoodeneffect.com*. Accessed January 6, 2026. https://www.thewoodeneffect.com/pyramid-of-success/.

Turner, Champ. "Mapping the Brazilian Amazon – The Roosevelt-Rondon Expedition of 1913-14." *Worlds Revealed: Geography & Maps at the Library of Congress*, July 18, 2025. https://blogs.loc.gov/maps/2025/07/mapping-the-brazilian-amazon-the-roosevelt-rondon-expedition-of-1913-14/.

▶ VIDEOS AND SPEAKING

Library of Congress. "Theodore Roosevelt - The River of Doubt, Part 1." YouTube video, uploaded by Library of Congress, January 4, 2010. https://www.youtube.com/watch?v=fKXOtJeaTEQ.

PBS. "Chapter 1 | Into the Amazon | American Experience | PBS." YouTube video, uploaded by American Experience | PBS, January 2, 2018. https://www.youtube.com/watch?v=JwJqj76V8PU.

TED. "The Difference Between Winning and Succeeding | John Wooden | TED." YouTube video, uploaded by TED, March 26, 2009. https://www.youtube.com/watch?v=0MMpsvqiG8.

"Teddy Roosevelt and the River of Doubt." YouTube video, uploaded by Daily Dose Documentary, September 22, 2023. https://www.youtube.com/watch?v=h2VGCXJBIS8.

▶ **INTERVIEWS AND PODCASTS**

Breen, Matt. "Teddy Roosevelt and the River of Doubt." *The Explorers Podcast* (podcast episodes), January 19, 2022. https://explorerspodcast.com/teddy-roosevelt/.

McVay, Sean. "Sean McVay Gets Candid on NFL Offenses, Puka Nacua, Matthew Stafford & More." YouTube video. Posted by *The Athletic Football Show*, July 23, 2024. https://www.youtube.com/watch?v=ainOTjr9SxQ.

Senra, David. "#175 Theodore Roosevelt's Darkest Journey." *Founders* (podcast episode), April 11, 2021. https://open.spotify.com/episode/4zrE3tLcMUsMCYHCt3ZrNh.

Carve Out: Pottery Class

▶ **BOOKS**

Bayles, David, and Ted Orland. *Art & Fear: Observations on the Perils (and Rewards) of Artmaking.* Image Continuum Press, 2001.

Chapter 5: The Way it's ~~Always~~ Never Been Done

▶ **BOOKS**

Berger, Eric. *Liftoff: Elon Musk and the Desperate Early Days That Launched SpaceX.* William Morrow, 2021.

Berger, Eric. *Reentry: SpaceX, Elon Musk, and the Reusable Rockets That Launched a Second Space Age.* William Morrow, 2024.

Cummings, E. E. "A Poet's Advice." In *A Miscellany Revised,* edited by George J. Firmage, 216. October House, 1965.

Dunnavant, Keith. *Montana: The Biography of Football's Joe Cool.* Thomas Dunne Books, 2015.

Glauber, *Guts and Genius.*

Harris, *The Genius.*

Hastings, Reed, and Erin Meyer. *No Rules Rules: Netflix and the Culture of Reinvention.* Penguin Press, 2020.

Hubbard, Elbert. "A Message to Garcia." *The Philistine* 9, no. 1, 1899.

Isaacson, Walter. *Elon Musk.* Simon & Schuster, 2023.

Knight, *Shoe Dog.*

McCord, *Patty. Powerful: Building a Culture of Freedom and Responsibility.* Silicon Guild, 2018.

Randolph, Marc. *That Will Never Work: The Birth of Netflix and the Amazing Life of an Idea.* Little, Brown and Company, 2019.

Vance, Ashlee. *Elon Musk: Tesla, SpaceX, and the Quest for a Fantastic Future.* Ecco, 2015.

Walsh, *Building a Champion.*

Sources

Walsh, *Finding the Winning Edge.*

Walsh, *The Score Takes Care of Itself.*

Zell, Sam. *Am I Being Too Subtle?: Straight Talk from a Business Rebel.* Portfolio, 2017.

▷ ARTICLES AND DOCUMENTS

Britannica Editors. "How Fast Was the Concorde Jet?" *Britannica.com.* Accessed January 6, 2026. https://www.britannica.com/technology/How-Fast-Was-the-Concorde-Jet.

Cowing, Keith. "SpaceX Falcon Launch Vehicle Unveiled in Washington D.C." *SpaceRef,* December 4, 2003. https://spaceref.com/uncategorized/spacex-falcon-launch-vehicle-unveiled-in-washington-dc/.

National Museums Scotland. "Concorde: The Story of Supersonic Passenger Flight." *National Museums Scotland Discover Catalogue.* Accessed January 6, 2026. https://www.nms.ac.uk/discover-catalogue/concorde-the-story-of-supersonic-passenger-flight.

Netflix. "Culture at Netflix." *Netflix Careers.* Accessed January 6, 2026. https://jobs.netflix.com/culture.

▷ INTERVIEWS AND PODCASTS

Senra, David. "#368 Elon Musk and the Culture of Founders." *Founders* (podcast episode), October 17, 2024. https://open.spotify.com/episode/2NO5YEUX3XOraWVTYXNnVv.

Senra, David. "369 Elon Musk and the Early Days of SpaceX." *Founders* (podcast episode), November 1, 2024. https://podcasts.apple.com/us/podcast/369-elon-musk-and-the-early-days-of-spacex/id1141877104?i=1000675400172.

Chapter 6: The Power of Constraints

▷ BOOKS

Chesterton, G.K. *Orthodoxy.* John Lane, 1908.

Darwin, Charles. *On the Origin of Species.* Macmillan Collector's Library, 2017.

Dunnavant, *Montana.*

Harris, *The Genius.*

Jones, Brian Jay. *Becoming Dr. Seuss: Theodor Geisel and the Making of an American Imagination.* Dutton, 2019.

Saint-Exupéry, Antoine de. *Airman's Odyssey.* Translated by Lewis Galantière. Reynal & Hitchcock, 1932.

Seuss, Dr. *Green Eggs and Ham.* Random House, 1960.

Walsh, *Finding the Winning Edge.*

Walsh, *The Score Takes Care of Itself.*

Young, Steve and Jeff Benedict. *QB: My Life Behind the Spiral.* Houghton Mifflin Harcourt, 2016.

▷ ARTICLES AND DOCUMENTS

Clear, James. "The Weird Strategy Dr. Seuss Used to Create His Greatest Work." *JamesClear.com.* Accessed January 6, 2026. https://jamesclear.com/dr-seuss.

Haught-Tromp, Catrinel. "The Green Eggs and Ham Hypothesis: How Constraints Facilitate Creativity." *Psychology of Aesthetics, Creativity, and the Arts* 11, no. 1: 10–17, 2017. https://www.cct.umb.edu/630/files/HaughtTromp2017-GreenEggsandHam.pdf.

Houke, Jon. "Raising Cane's Is Launching 6 Restaurants in June. Here's the List." *RetailWire,* June 4, 2025. https://retailwire.com/raising-canes-6-restaurants-list/.

McCue, T.J. "6 Lessons From Dr. Seuss." *Forbes*, January 1, 2013.https://www.forbes.com/sites/tjmccue/2013/01/01/6-lessons-from-dr-seuss/.

Monceaux, Ryan. "Bill Yeoman Introduces The Veer Offense." *GoCoogs.com*, October 23, 2025. https://gocoogs.com/bill-yeoman-veer-offense/.

National Inventors Hall of Fame. "The Invention of the Post-it Note." *Invent.org*, June 5, 2020. https://www.invent.org/blog/trends-stem/who-invented-post-it-notes.SI Staff. "Zone Read Still Giving Defenses Fits." Sports Illustrated, September 25, 2014.https://www.si.com/college/2014/09/25/ap-fbc-zone-read.

Staples, Andy. "His Innovative Offense Now the Norm, Rich Rodriguez Must Keep Evolving." *Sports Illustrated*, July 23, 2014. https://www.si.com/college/2014/07/24/arizona-wildcats-rich-rodriguez-pac-12-media-days.

▶ VIDEOS AND SPEAKING

University of California. "How Dr. Seuss Created Green Eggs and Ham." YouTube video, uploaded by Fig. 1 by University of California, December 23, 2014. https://www.youtube.com/watch?v=jUkfO-TAOLY.

▶ INTERVIEWS AND PODCASTS

Kulps, Jason. "165. From Chicken Fingers to One of the Richest People in the World! Raising Cane's Founder and CEO Todd Graves Reveals His Path to Building the Wildly Popular Restaurant." *Trading Secrets* (podcast episode), May 13, 2024. https://open.spotify.com/episode/4Ihkmfhu9hL2QvdbsPD4oF.

Raz, Guy. "Raising Cane's: Todd Graves." *How I Built This with Guy Raz* (podcast episode), April 25, 2022. https://podcasts.apple.com/us/podcast/raising-canes-todd-graves/id1150510297?i=1000557743745.

Senra, David. "#383 Todd Graves and His $10 Billion Chicken Finger Dream." *Founders* (podcast episode), March 17, 2025. https://open.spotify.com/episode/3yYOXaRLtp0WQ7Xo886z8u.

Von, Theo. "Raising Cane's Founder Todd Graves." *This Past Weekend with Theo Von* (podcast episode), May 18, 2021. https://podcasts.apple.com/ca/podcast/raising-canes-founder-todd-graves/id1190981360?i=1000522147428.

Welles, Orson. *Quotations attributed to Orson Welles*. Various interviews from 1950-1970.

Chapter 7: Be the Expert

▶ BOOKS

Clear, James. *Atomic Habits: An Easy & Proven Way to Build Good Habits & Break Bad Ones*. Avery, 2018.

Ericsson, K. Anders, and Robert Pool. *Peak: Secrets from the New Science of Expertise*. Houghton Mifflin Harcourt, 2016.

Gladwell, Malcolm. *Outliers: The Story of Success*. Little, Brown and Company, 2008.

Harris, *The Genius*.

Ladouceur, Bob. *Chasing Perfection: A Coach's Journey to Honor, Victory, and the Greatest Team in History*. Houghton Mifflin Harcourt, 2014.

Lowenstein, Roger. *Buffett: The Making of an American Capitalist*. Random House, 1995.

Schroeder, Alice. *The Snowball: Warren Buffett and the Business of Life*. Bantam Books, 2008.

Sun Tzu. *The Art of War*. Translated by Samuel B. Griffith. Oxford University Press, 1963.

Walsh, *Building a Champion*.

Walsh, *Finding the Winning Edge*.

Sources

Walsh, *The Score Takes Care of Itself.*

Willis, Chris. *A Nearly Perfect Season: The Inside Story of the 1984 San Francisco 49ers.* St. Martin's Press, 2006.

Wooden, John. *Practical Modern Basketball.* Prentice-Hall, 1966.

▶ ARTICLES AND DOCUMENTS

75th Ranger Regiment Public Affairs. "Under Heavy Fire, Ranger Medics Save Lives with Blood Donations." *Army.mil,* January 27, 2020. https://www.army.mil/article/231597/ under_heavy_fire_ranger_medics_save_lives_with_blood_donations.

Buffett, Warren E. "Berkshire Hathaway Inc. Shareholder Letter, 2014." *Berkshire Hathaway* Archive (Memorex). Accessed January 8, 2026. https://berkshire.memorex.ai/viewer /21bc3eca-0b41-4e36-87d6-47dd61757041.

Eyland, Gísli. "The Salad Oil Scandal of 1963." *Fundamental Finance Playbook.* August 26, 2020. https://fundamentalfinanceplaybook.com/histories/the-salad-oil-scandal-of-1963/.

Mayne, Maj. Tony. "Ranger Whole Blood Program Wins an Army's Greatest Innovation Award." *Army.mil,* March 14, 2017. https://www.army.mil/article/184219/ranger_ whole_blood_program_wins_an_armys_greatest_innovation_award.

Rohn, Jim. "The Formula for Success and Failure." *Jim Rohn Blog.* July 12, 2019. https:// www.jimrohn.com/the-formula-for-success-and-failure.

Song, K. H., et al. "Ranger O Low Titer (ROLO): Whole Blood Transfusion for Tactical Combat Casualty Care." *Military Medicine* 188, no. 7–8: e2733–e2737, 2023. https:// academic.oup.com/milmed/article/188/7-8/e2733/6424990?login=false.

Stegall, Sgt. Sarah. "Valkyrie: Emergency Fresh Whole Blood Transfusion Enhances 15th MEU Medical Capabilities." *Marines.mil,* February 2, 2021. https://www.marines. mil/News/News-Display/Article/2489777/valkyrie-emergency-fresh-whole-blood-transfusion-enhances-15th-meu-medical-capa/.

U.S. Army. "Ranger Creed." *Army.mil.* Accessed January 6, 2026. https://www.army.mil/ values/ranger.html.

@CCignettiIU (Curt Cignetti). "@ JMU , I had to stalk complacency because of our success. @ IU, I am stalking softness & will eliminate it in every area , so that we have the opportunity to stalk complacency.." *X,* September 27, 2024. https://x.com/ CCignettiIU/status/1746139253438824764.

▶ INTERVIEWS AND PODCASTS

Buffett, Warren. "Warren Buffett's Most Legendary Interview Ever!" *Motivation2Invest* (podcast episode), accessed January 7, 2026. https://open.spotify.com/episode/ 4HY3yoaj61tDttENkXc69e.

Grieve, Kyle. "TIP733: How Warren Buffett Became Warren Buffett." *We Study Billionaires - The Investor's Podcast Network* (podcast episode), June 28, 2025. https:// podcasts.apple.com/us/podcast/tip733-how-warren-buffett-became-warren-buffett/ id928933489?i=1000714961582.

Carve Out: Fire and Forget

▶ ARTICLES AND DOCUMENTS

"Javelin Light Forces Anti-Tank Guided Weapon (LF-ATGW)." *DefenseAdvancement.com.* Accessed January 8, 2026. https://www.defenseadvancement.com/projects/javelin-light-forces-anti-tank-guided-weapon-lf-atgw/.

U.S. Army. "TOW." *Redstone Arsenal Historical Information.* Accessed January 7, 2026. https://history.redstone.army.mil/miss-tow.html.

Chapter 8: The *Right* People

▶ **BOOKS**

Bryant, *Bear.*

Collins, *Good to Great.*

Dent, *The Junction Boys.*

Dunnavant, *Montana.*

Gerstner, Louis V., Jr. *Who Says Elephants Can't Dance?: Leading a Great Enterprise Through Dramatic Change.* HarperBusiness, 2002.

Harris, *The Genius.*

Isaacson, Walter. *Steve Jobs.* Simon & Schuster, 2011.

Jager, Rama Dev, and Rafael Ortiz. *In the Company of Giants: Candid Conversations with the Visionaries of the Digital World.* McGraw-Hill, 1997.

Rice, Jerry, with Brian Curtis. *Go Long!: My Journey Beyond the Game and the Fame.* Villard, 2007.

Talty, *The Leadership Secrets of Nick Saban.*

Walsh, *Building a Champion.*

Walsh, *Finding the Winning Edge.*

Walsh, *The Score Takes Care of Itself.*

▶ **ARTICLES AND DOCUMENTS**

Hession, Joe. "49ers Museum's Artifact of the Month: Draft Day in April." *Levi's Stadium*, April 22, 2015. https://levisstadium.com/2015/04/49ers-museums-artifact-of-the-month-draft-day-in-april/.

Schwantes, Marcel. "This 32-Year-Old Steve Jobs Quote May Be His Best Leadership Lesson Ever." *Inc.*, October 11, 2024. https://www.inc.com/marcel-schwantes/this-32-year-old-steve-jobs-quote-may-be-his-best-leadership-lesson-ever/90986760.

▶ **VIDEOS AND SPEAKING**

Buffett, Warren. "Warren Buffett - What We Look For In Hiring People." YouTube short video, uploaded by RETMedia, November 23, 2022. https://www.youtube.com/shorts/4QmyT5PZdFA.

▶ **INTERVIEWS AND PODCASTS**

Clark, Josh, and Chuck Bryant. "The Wright Brothers" *Stuff You Should Know* (podcast episode), January 7, 2021. https://open.spotify.com/episode/100oSESY3qoAV8e237SsQN.

Feith, Greg, and John Goglia. "Episode 71 – Tribute to Charles Taylor, the Father of Aircraft Maintenance." *Flight Safety Detectives* (podcast episode), May 27, 2021. https://flightsafetydetectives.com/tribute-to-charles-taylor-the-father-of-aircraft-maintenance-episode-71/.

Guy Raz. "IBM: Lou Gerstner." *Wisdom From The Top with Guy Raz* (podcast episode), July 27, 2022. https://podcasts.apple.com/us/podcast/ibm-lou-gerstner/id1460154838?i=1000564856249.

Knowledge at Wharton Staff. "Lou Gerstner's Turnaround Tales at IBM." *Knowledge at Wharton Podcast* (podcast episode), December 18, 2002. https://knowledge.wharton.upenn.edu/podcast/knowledge-at-wharton-podcast/lou-gerstners-turnaround-tales-at-ibm/.

Wood, Chris. "Episode 96 – Put a Hemi in It: Wright Brothers Part 3." *Oral Presentations* (podcast episode), June 3, 2022. https://podcasts.apple.com/gb/podcast/episode-96-put-a-hemi-in-it-wright -brothers-part-3/id1490806721?i=1000565159897.

Chapter 9: Fast and Flat

▷ BOOKS

Catmull, Ed, with Amy Wallace. Creativity, Inc.: *Overcoming the Unseen Forces That Stand in the Way of True Inspiration.* Random House, 2014.

Dalio, Ray. *Principles: Life and Work.* Simon & Schuster, 2017.

Harris, *The Genius.*

Knight, *Shoe Dog.*

McChrystal, Stanley. *My Share of the Task: A Memoir.* Portfolio/Penguin, 2013.

McChrystal, Stanley. *On Character: Choices That Define a Life.* Portfolio/Penguin, 2025.

McChrystal, Stanley, with Tantum Collins, David Silverman, and Chris Fussell. *Team of Teams: New Rules of Engagement for a Complex World.* Portfolio/Penguin, 2015.

Naylor, Sean. *Relentless Strike: The Secret History of Joint Special Operations Command.* St. Martin's Press, 2015.

Price, David A. *The Pixar Touch: The Making of a Company.* Alfred A. Knopf, 2008.

Taleb, Nassim Nicholas. *Skin in the Game: Hidden Asymmetries in Daily Life.* Random House, 2018.

Walsh, *Building a Champion.*

Walsh, *Finding the Winning Edge.*

Walsh, *The Score Takes Care of Itself.*

Young and Mitchell, *QB.*

▷ ARTICLES AND DOCUMENTS

Branson, Richard. "How to Lead the Next Generation." *Virgin.com* (Richard Branson blog), October 10, 2017. https://www.virgin.com/branson-family/richard-branson-blog/how-lead-next-generation.

Catmull, Ed. "Inside the Pixar Braintrust." *Fast Company,* March 12, 2014. https://www.fast company.com/3027135/inside-the-pixar-braintrust.

Netflix. "Culture at Netflix."

Teslik, Lee Hudson. "Profile: Abu Musab al-Zarqawi." *Council on Foreign Relations.* June 8, 2006. https://www.cfr.org/backgrounder/profile-abu-musab-al-zarqawi.

▷ VIDEOS AND SPEAKING

ENDEVR. *Black Ops: The Takedown of Iraq's Most Wanted Terrorist | Al-Zarqawi | ENDEVR Documentary.* YouTube video, uploaded by ENDEVR, February 21, 2025. https://www.youtube.com/watch?v=xr-WUy_E-Rc.

Walsh, Bill. "Bill Walsh Hall of Fame Speech 1993." YouTube video, uploaded by 80s Football Cards, April 9, 2023. https://www.youtube.com/watch?v=v1AZ00j6MVk.

▷ INTERVIEWS AND PODCASTS

Grant, Adam. "How Pixar's Ed Catmull and Pete Docter make magic on and off screen." *ReThinking* (podcast episode), August 4, 2023. https://www.youtube.com/watch?v=W4o6Ufot-Dc.

Parrish, Shane. "#132 Ret. Gen. Stanley McChrystal - The Essence of Leadership." *The Knowledge Project* (podcast episode), March 8, 2022. https://podcasts.apple.com/us/ podcast/132-ret-gen-stanley-mcchrystal-the-essence-of-leadership/id990149481?i=1000553265173.

Chapter 10: Do Unto Others

▷ **BOOKS**

Harris, *The Genius.*

Dunnavant, *Montana.*

Meadow's Edge Group, LLC, comp. *Life Wisdom: Quotes from John Maxwell: Insights on Leadership.* B&H Publishing Group, 2014.

Walsh, *Building a Champion.*

Walsh, *Finding the Winning Edge.*

Walsh, *The Score Takes Care of Itself.*

Young and Mitchell, *QB.*

▷ **ARTICLES AND DOCUMENTS**

ESPN.com. "Greatest NFL Coaches – Bill Walsh Coaching Tree." *ESPN*, June 10, 2013. https://www.espn.com/nfl/story/_/page/coachingtreewalsh130610/greatest-nfl-coaches-bill-walsh-coaching-tree.

Theeuwen, Hailey A., and Anthony W. Kim. "Commentary: Perception Is Reality, but Reality Is How You Make Them Feel." *JTCVS* Open 8: 522–523, October 27, 2021. https://pmc.ncbi.nlm.nih.gov/articles/PMC9390472/.

The Timeline

Refer to chapter citations.

Bill Walsh's Standard of Performance

Walsh, *The Score Takes Care of Itself.*

Leadership Library

The work doesn't end here.

Scan the QR code above to access the
Bring Your Own Pencil Leadership Library,
an evolving collection of tools, references,
and resources.

BRINGYOUROWNPENCIL.COM/
PAGES/LEADERSHIP-LIBRARY

About the Authors

Dan Casey is a football coach, strategist, and writer. Known for his obsessive curiosity and clarity of thought, he has spent more than a decade studying football at its deepest levels – schemes, structure, decision-making, and the hidden margins where games are actually won. Through coaching, teaching, writing, and film study, he has earned the trust of coaches at every level of football, including opportunities to collaborate with and learn alongside NFL staffs. His work is defined by an uncommon ability to see the game both technically and philosophically, and to explain it in ways that make others better.

Dan represents a modern evolution of football leadership: one rooted in shared knowledge, disciplined preparation, and respect for the craft. He has become a bridge between generations of coaches, translating complex concepts into practical tools while honoring the foundational principles that built the sport. More than tactics, his work emphasizes standards – how teams prepare, how leaders think, and how culture is built over time. *Bring Your Own Pencil* reflects that same ethos: a belief that success in football, as in life, is earned through intention, curiosity, and relentless attention to detail.

You can learn more about his recent projects at
COACHDANCASEY.COM

Griffin Brand is an entrepreneur, investor, and former Army Ranger. He graduated from Davidson College, where he played football, before spending more than eight years on active duty in the U.S. Army, including service in Europe and later in Special Operations with the elite 75th Ranger Regiment. After leaving the military, Griffin transitioned into private equity, first as Director of Investor Relations for Wellings Capital and then as Vice President of Corporate Development at HighGround Restoration Group, a private equity–backed company focused on acquiring and scaling damage restoration businesses across the United States.

Driven by the pursuit of personal excellence and a desire to help others grow, Griffin co-founded the Veteran Ventures Podcast, which shares the stories of veterans who have successfully transitioned into business and entrepreneurship. His work sits at the intersection of leadership, discipline, and building a life aligned with purpose. Based in North Carolina, he and his family spend their time traveling, staying active outdoors, and investing in experiences that matter.

Learn more about Griffin's work at
GRIFFINBRAND.COM